The Nine Lives of Charles E. Lively:

The Deadliest Man in the West Virginia-Colorado Coal Mine Wars

Also by R.G. Yoho:

Return to Matewan

Long Ride to Yesterday

Boot Hill Valley

Death Comes to Redhawk

Death Rides the Rail

Nightfall Over Nicodemus

The Evil Day

America's History is His Story!

Major Impact

Palo Duro

The Nine Lives of Charles E. Lively:

The Deadliest Man in the West Virginia-Colorado Coal Mine Wars

R.G. Yoho

FOX RUN
PUBLISHING
QUALITY PUBLISHING ONE BOOK AT A TIME

Publisher's Cataloging-in-Publication Data
provided by Five Rainbows Cataloging Services

Names: Yoho, R. G., author. | Powers, Fred M., writer of foreword.
Title: The nine lives of Charles E. Lively : the deadliest man in the West Virginia-
    Colorado coal mine wars / R. G. Yoho ; [foreword by] Fred M. Powers.
Description: Burlington, NC : Fox Run Publishing, 2020. | Includes bibliographical
    references and index.
Identifiers: LCCN 2020933641 (print) | ISBN 978-1-945602-10-8 (hardcover) |
    ISBN 978-1-945602-11-5 (paperback)
Subjects: LCSH: Coal Strike, W. Va., 1920-1921. | Coal Strike, Colo., 1913-1914. |
    West Virginia Mine Wars, W. Va., 1897-1921. | Coal miners--West Virginia--
    History. | Coal miners--Colorado--History. | Baldwin-Felts Detectives, Inc.--
    Biography. | BISAC: BIOGRAPHY & AUTOBIOGRAPHY / Historical. |
    HISTORY / Modern / 20th Century.
Classification: LCC HD8039.M615 Y64 2020 (print) | LCC HD8039.M615
    (ebook) | DDC 622/.334--dc23.

Cover design by Sandra Miller Linhart

Published by
Fox Run Publishing LLC
2779 South Church Street, #305
Burlington, NC 27215
http://www.foxrunpub.com/

To Bill and Dave...
See you both at breakfast.

Table of Contents

List of Images

Acknowledgments

Since I am primarily a Western novelist, the list of things I don't really know about undertaking a work of this magnitude would...well, fill a book.

Writing books is similar to being a pitcher in Major League baseball. It's a solitary exercise, but you generally enjoy a much greater level of success when you have a great team behind you. And I have certainly been blessed to be surrounded by a great team.

I barely know where to begin thanking all those who have done something to help me with this work. Perhaps most of all, I fear that I will forget someone. If you've contributed help or insights to this author, and I've failed to mention you, please accept my apologies. Any oversight from me certainly wasn't intentional.

First of all, I am supported by a kind, attractive, and loving wife, who is both my best friend and most trusted advisor. On top of all that, she's just doggone cute to look at. If that wasn't enough, JoEllen is also an outstanding photographer, her talents are largely self-taught. The pictures you see of me on my book covers have all been taken by her. A number of the photos in this book also came from her hands.

Obviously, I want to thank Keith Jones and the folks at Fox Run for their confidence in me, their hard work on my behalf, and their dedication to getting this story out. I appreciate Hailey Bibbee, who worked with me on editing. I must also say that the cover art by Sandra Linhart for this book was superb.

Sheriff Jim Wilson offered me his knowledge of ballistics, his many years of expertise as a lawman, and his crucial insights into human behavior, knowledge that comes from one of the finest Texas gentlemen you'd ever hope to meet.

Therese Bombardiere generously employed her years of experience and training in psychology, consenting to add her expertise to this work, to help analyze Charles E. Lively's behavior and mental state.

I want to thank all the good people at the Huerfano County (Colorado) Historical Society, Huerfano Heritage Center, and the Walsenburg (Colorado) Mining Museum, Carolyn Newman, Sharon Vezzani, John Van Keuran, and others who serve there.

Another valuable asset to this work was Becky Kaufman, who works at the Eastern Regional Coal Archives at Bluefield, West Virginia.

My friend, Randy Marcum, at the West Virginia State Archives has supplied me with information and given me tips which often led me down the road to other discoveries on Lively. Moreover, while I'm on the subject of the State Archives, I also want to give a shout out to Aaron Parson, who helped with a number of the pictures I used in this book.

As a native of the city, I must give credit to those who live and work in Parkersburg, West Virginia, a special place I will always call home. I couldn't have done this without them. Jim Miracle, at the Parkersburg-Wood County Library, supplied me with information that was absolutely priceless to this story. A special word of thanks also goes to those in the Contemporary Writers Group, Kathryn McClead, Cole Smith, and Kim Scott, for their reading and editing suggestions.

Throughout this process, I've been especially blessed to become friends with Wess Harris, author of "Written in Blood," who was a close friend of William C. Blizzard, whose dad led the Redneck Army. Along with being a walking encyclopedia on the coal mine wars in general, and Bill Blizzard in particular, Wess has given me some critical advice.

Another priceless friendship I've made upon this journey has been with James Baldwin, great grandson of William G. Baldwin, of Baldwin-Felts. James has graciously provided me with a number of observations into the Baldwin-Felts Detective Agency and its leadership.

My chats with Lucia St. Clair Robson, one of the world's finest historical novelists and my good friend, helped me to determine the best approach to telling Charles E. Lively's story.

I want to thank my friend and former coal miner, Fred Powers, for penning the Foreword for this book. Others who offered their talents or in some way gave their assistance to this project were Chris Enss, Eliot Parker, Teri Hazlett, Doug Estepp, Eric Wittenberg, Dale Schofield, and Terry Harrison.

As I said earlier, if I have forgotten anyone, please accept my apology. I am, however, grateful to everyone who helped me to bring the compelling story of this central figure in the coal mine wars to life.

R. G. Yoho

Foreword

This long-overdue book of the American industrial spy and alleged assassin, "Charles E. Lively," of the Baldwin-Felts detective Agency which you are about to partake upon, will give you insights into the tipping points of the West Virginia Mine Wars at Matewan and Welch. These events led to "The Battle of Blair Mountain," the largest insurrection mounted on American soil since the "Civil War." The Mine Wars began at 'Paint Creek and Cabin Creek' in 1912 and ended with subsequent murder trials in 1922. The 100th Anniversary of this vastly important American Labor War for economic betterment is upon us and is written in the blood of its working citizens.

The small populated state of West Virginia with its vast reserves of 'Coal' became the forefront of union organizing activity throughout the early part of twentieth century America. The lengthy mine wars that West Virginia and Colorado (1913-1914) experienced were fought by workers against the agents of the mine owners and the business-friendly interests of state governments. The man involved in hindering both states' struggle for basic humane worker rights and unionization was C. E. Lively. The plight of the miners who were killed in exorbitant numbers from unsafe working conditions and their families living in decrepit 'coal camps' is an American story. The resistance initiated by the United Mine Workers for union representation bears witness and testimony to the American Labor Movement, of which we now enjoy the benefits of the world's most powerful economy.

The life of this man, C.E. Lively, has been thoroughly researched by Mr. R.G. Yoho, author of several western novels and President of West Virginia Writers. He is now ready to present to the world a book-length work chronologizing the circumstances leading to Mr. Lively's vocation as an industrial spy within the ranks of miners and the deadly violence perpetrated by his actions upon the American laborer.

My friendship with Mr. Yoho came about when conversing with him at a couple of writer's workshops that I attended. I could feel his compassion for the miners as we became acquaintances. My background is of being a native West Virginian who was reared up in a 'coal camp' and a small working mining town in McDowell County. My decision at twenty years old was to follow my dad's vocation to become a UMWA underground miner. My goal was also to become a teacher and I accomplished this while working in the mines. In retirement now, I have become a coal mining storyteller and writer with self-published memoirs of my coalfield youth and mining experiences.

Fred "Powerhouse" Powers

Introduction

In researching this book, one quickly learns that there are many spellings—or misspellings—for the names contained in this work.

In fact, there is no shortage of names and spellings for the subject of this book, Charles E. Lively. Now, while some of the written accounts on this man may have been simple errors in spelling or mistakes in reporting, it is quite likely that some of those variations may have been by design, alterations Lively himself used to conceal his real identity from those he sought to investigate. The name might also have been altered to conceal his identity from those who were likely to seek Lively's death for those instances where he betrayed their trust.

Charles E. Lively has used or been identified by the name Everett, Everet, Evert, and even once by the name of Charles Lester. One prominent news story even identified him as Ernest Lively.

The initial accounts of this man show him going by Everett Lively, which was most likely his birth name. In all reality, there is some evidence that the name "Charles" may have simply been a moniker of Lively's own creation.

In conducting the research, there is also a multitude of reasons to believe that Lively went by numerous other aliases as well. In reading this account, you will quickly discover that Lively indeed had much to hide. There was also no shortage of enemies who wanted Lively dead.

In addition, there are no fewer than four different spellings for the name of Lively's mother. Therefore, in deference to him, this book will use only Charles' own version of his mother's name, Ameretta, which he listed on his World War II draft registration.

In conducting my research, I discovered there are also multiple spellings for the name of Charles E. Lively's wife, Icie. Throughout this work, I have deliberately chosen to go with the name used by the woman's children on her obituary and on her tombstone.

Charles E. Lively. Probably taken during his time out West.
(West Virginia State Archives)

CHAPTER 1

A Rendezvous with Destiny

On the morning of August 1, 1921, Baldwin-Felts Detective Charles E. Lively was waiting alongside the courthouse steps in Welch, West Virginia. As all the pictures of the man indicate, his manner of dress was impeccable. Lively usually wore a coat, all the better to hide the pair of guns he always carried, which he often shot with either hand. In most West Virginia towns in the early twentieth century, it was generally illegal to carry guns without a license. Lively, however, paid no heed to those laws, and the record reflects his numerous arrests on weapons charges. Underneath his coat that morning, he carried his pair of trusty, fully-loaded revolvers.[1] According to a reporter who knew him, the blue-eyed Lively was "an undersized man of slight build," but he was "alive with nervous energy." His gaze was also described as "shrewd, ever vigilant." The reporter also observed that Lively's "aquiline nose gives his face a hawkish touch," and like a hawk, Lively watched for his prey. The detective, used to going about his missions alone, wasn't going solo on this assignment.[2] There was too much at stake. Lively would have help, assisted by a number of other detectives nearby, each of them focused on the same primary objective, to pass out a death sentence to one specific individual, the former Matewan, West Virginia, Chief of Police, William Sidney Hatfield.

The record isn't clear whether Lively had any direct knowledge of the others' involvement in this conspiracy; it is reasonable, however, to speculate that he did. As Lively sat on the balustrade, engaged in a conversation with "a colored man," George Washington "Buster" Pence was also standing at the top of the steps, cleaning his nails with a pocket knife, waiting for Sid Hatfield's arrival.[3] Bill Salter, an agent who survived the

---

1. *Bluefield Daily Telegraph*, Bluefield, West Virginia, December 17, 1921.
2. S.D. Weyer, *The Cedar Rapids Evening Gazette*, Cedar Rapids, Iowa, August 6, 1921.
3. *Bluefield Daily Telegraph*, Bluefield, West Virginia, August 6, 1921.
   Gettysburg Times, Gettysburg, Pennsylvania, December 17, 1921.

Matewan Massacre by hiding in a trash can, was purportedly still inside the courthouse; however, despite Salter's location, he clearly was on the scene when the trouble started. Another loyal and trusted Baldwin-Felts agent, Hughey Lucas, was there on the lawn as well. All of the agents were armed and dangerous.[4]

There was a threat of rain in the air. Some of the locals carried umbrellas at the ivy-covered McDowell County Courthouse on that Monday morning. Charles was a man on a mission, and on that day, he was seeking to finally avenge the death of Albert Felts. Albert hadn't only been the late brother of Thomas Lafayette Felts, who was the vice president of the Baldwin-Felts Detective Agency, but Albert had also been like a brother to Charles E. Lively. It is believed that most of what Charles knew about being a secret service detective for the agency, he learned from his mentor, Albert. Charles even named one of his own sons after him, uniting their names as Charles Albert. It is certain that Lively didn't believe his trusted friend and fellow agent deserved to die in the manner he did, brutally shot down by a mob of militant miners and his sworn enemy, Sid Hatfield.

While Lively worked on his assignments in the western United States, Albert had often been his only confidant and his most trusted friend. In fact, he was often Lively's only connection to his home back in West Virginia. A little over one year before though, on May 19, 1920, Sid Hatfield and the other co-defendants killed Albert Felts, Albert's brother, Lee, and five other detectives. The armed citizens shot the detectives, fired multiple slugs into their bodies to make sure they were dead, and left their bloody, lifeless bodies to stain the streets of Matewan for several hours afterward.

In the days that followed, Sid often bragged about killing Albert; he laughed about it. Sid obviously gloried in the deed. Albert's death, along with that of his brother, Lee, and the killing of the five other detectives, made Hatfield a folk hero among union coal miners nationwide. The striking miners of Matewan, evicted from their homes by Baldwin-Felts, regarded 'Two-Gun Sid' as their personal champion, a knight in shining armor. The United Mine Workers of America had even featured

---

4. John A. Velke, "The True Story of the Baldwin-Felts Detective Agency," (Self-Published, 2004), p. 232. *Bluefield Daily Telegraph*, Bluefield, West Virginia, December 17, 1921. Howard Lee, "Bloodletting in Appalachia, The Story of West Virginia's Four Major Mine Wars and Other Thrilling Incidents of its Coal Fields," (West Virginia University Press, 1969), p. 68.

Hatfield in their 1920 film 'Smilin' Sid,' a reenactment of the shooting in Matewan.

When Hatfield was acquitted for the killing of Albert and Legrand "Lee" Felts, there was every reason to suspect that Thomas Felts wasn't satisfied to simply let the verdict stand. Moreover, Felts already plainly stated that he wanted the former Chief of Police to be "hanged by the neck."[5] Although there is still no conclusive evidence of his direct involvement, the events that followed Hatfield's verdict strongly suggest that Thomas Felts arranged for Sid to be indicted on a set of specious charges and face trial in McDowell County, a place "where the guards could safely take summary vengeance for the Matewan killings," according to a circuit court judge, I.C. Herndon.[6] When called upon to carry out this act of open and bloody retribution, Lively apparently did not balk at lending his gun skills to the boss, the grieving brother of his late friend, Albert.

Charles E. Lively had arrived in Welch early that morning, even boarding the same train with Sid Hatfield in the town of Iaeger, West Virginia. Upon entering the passenger car, "a man not easily fazed by situations that would disturb most people, Lively offered the Hatfield party a perfunctory greeting and then took a seat next to Kirkpatrick," the friend and deputy sheriff tasked with protecting Sid Hatfield's life.[7] However, forty-five minutes later, once their train reached the city of Welch, the time for insincere pleasantries was over. Both Lively and Hatfield had places they needed to be and appointments they needed to keep.

Unable to get a room in the crowded city of Welch, Hatfield went to the Ellwood Hotel room of his attorney, C.J. Van Fleet, who invited them to rest and wait for their court appearance there. At the urging of his attorney, Hatfield agreed to leave his revolvers behind in the room, unlike his earlier criminal trial in Williamson, where it was discovered Sid brought his guns with him into the courtroom. Ed Chambers, Hatfield's friend and co-defendant in Albert's death, who accompanied Sid on this trip, also consented to leave his gun at the hotel. At 10:30 in the morning, the train whistle blew, signaling the arrival of another train from the Norfolk & Western. The train whistle was also the signal for Sid and the others to leave the hotel room and make their way over to the courthouse to meet with his attorney,

---

5. *Muskogee Times Democrat*, Muskogee, Oklahoma, September 16, 1920.
6. Lee, "Bloodletting in Appalachia," p. 70.
7. Robert Shogan, "The Battle of Blair Mountain: The Story of America's Largest Labor Uprising," (Westview Press, 2004), p. 156.

who just successfully argued for a change of venue. The trial was to be moved to Greenbrier County, a more favorable location for the defendant, Sid Hatfield, to receive justice and a less favorable location for his enemies, who wished to see him killed or convicted.[8]

In the distance, Charles E. Lively saw Sid and his wife, Jessie, the former Mrs. Testerman, the late mayor's wife, walking slowly up the sidewalk towards the majestic stone courthouse. Armed and ready, Lively waited for them there. The McDowell County Courthouse sat high upon a hill, almost a focal point for the city of Welch, offering a clear vantage point from which a person could see many of the activities taking place nearby. Down from the courthouse, a high stone wall ran the length of the hillside, like a fat man's belt, straining to keep the bulging belly of earth from spilling over onto the sidewalk, along Wyoming Street. This enabled a person walking along the sidewalk to travel up those first set of steps, which ran parallel to it and reach the initial landing, before making a sharp turn to continue up the final set of steps to the courthouse. For those standing next to the courthouse, the steepness of the hillside would also temporarily block their view of anyone just starting up the steps, which led directly into this West Virginia hall of justice. But on that dreary, Monday morning, there would be no justice in West Virginia, just vengeance.

There was a great throng of people gathered on the courthouse lawn that day. A few of them were well-wishers, ones who had come to show their support for Sid. Others were court jurors, on a recess, waiting for court to reconvene.[9] Many of those assembled in front of the courthouse, including state policemen and McDowell County deputies,[10] were only there to assist in Lively's mission, or to provide favorable testimony for the agents' bogus and eventual claims of self-defense.[11]

Perhaps the most damning and shameful fact of all is that the State Police, then known as the West Virginia Department of Public Safety, which had their Detachment Headquarters located

8. James Green, "The Devil is Here in These Hills, West Virginia's Coal Miners and Their Battle for Freedom," (Atlantic Monthly Press, 2015), p. 245, *Bluefield Daily Telegraph*, Bluefield, West Virginia, August 4, 1921, William C. Blizzard, Wess Harris, ed., "When Miners March," (PM Press, 2010), p. 140.
9. *Bluefield Daily Telegraph*, Bluefield, West Virginia, December 14, 1921.
10. Velke, "The True Story of the Baldwin-Felts Detective Agency," p. 231.
11. *Bluefield Daily Telegraph*, Bluefield, West Virginia, December 14, 1921. John Velke, "The True Story of the Baldwin-Felts Detective Agency." Lee, Howard, "Bloodletting in Appalachia."

in the city, apparently looked the other way and did absolutely nothing to ensure the safety of Hatfield and Chambers, thereby making the State Police complicit in the actions of Lively and the other agents.[12] "At the head of the steps were Lively, Pence, Lucas, (Robert) Day, L.H. Ellis, a state policeman; C.M. Samson and B.C. Gallamore. The latter was sitting on the right side of the steps. There were a number of jurors in the court yard near the head of the steps. Just across the street was Walter Mitchell, chief of police of Welch."[13] Multiple Baldwin-Felts agents and those loyal to Thomas Felts were stationed all around the courthouse. This was not destined to be a gun battle; this was strictly an assassination.

Ed and Sallie Chambers started up the steps first, with Sid and his wife following not too far behind them. Upon reaching the first landing of the staircase, Sid spoke to a couple of well-wishers in the crowd and lifted his hand to wave. That was the moment for which Lively had been waiting. He and the other agents sprang into action, drew their guns, and rushed towards their unsuspecting victims. A fusillade of shots rang out. Men were bloodied and fell...

The story of Charles E. Lively is one of great mystery, deception, and violence. Perhaps no book can ever fully capture this enigma of a man, but this one will largely chronicle the detective's life, not only from his own words, but also from the vast array of public records and news accounts. "Lively is a quiet sort of chap—not in the least what one would picture in his imagination as a gunman, but his life while a secret service man for nine years in the employ of the Baldwin-Felts Agency reads like chapters from the most thrilling 'penny dreadful' ever written, and covers territory stretching from the battle-scarred hills of the Colorado strike zone to the blood-drenched valleys along the Tug River."[14] Although the events and violence of the coal mine wars in both West Virginia and Colorado have been told and retold by any number of talented authors, an understanding of those events can never fully take place without an exhaustive study of the life of Charles E. Lively, one of its most prominent and infamous figures.

---

12. James Green, "The Devil is Here in These Hills, West Virginia's Coal Miners and Their Battle for Freedom," p. 181, 182. To further buttress this point, Green stated: "...West Virginia legislators created a new state police force on the grounds that without such a constabulary the Mountain State might become a haven for Bolsheviks and anarchists."
13. *Bluefield Daily Telegraph*, Bluefield, West Virginia, August 2, 1921.
14. *Bluefield Daily Telegraph*, Bluefield, West Virginia, August 6, 1921.

Matewan Police Chief Sid Hatfield. Known as "Smiling Sid" and "Two-Gun Sid," Hatfield was a folk hero among union coal miners.

(West Virginia State Archives)

CHAPTER 2
A Lively Arrival

"'In the western country,' Thomas Jefferson wrote in his *Notes on Virginia* in 1785, 'coal is known to be in so many places, as to have induced an opinion that the whole tract between the Laurel Mountains and Ohio yields coal.'"[1] Coal was indeed abundant in the region, but there was no efficient or economical method to get it out of the state. The proliferation of the railroads changed that, as rugged mountains gave way to equally-rugged men, who, through the sweat of their brows, tunneled their way through these great stone obstacles. Tracks were laid throughout the state and that once isolated area became accessible to bold and wealthy men, such as Collis P. Huntington, "who needed West Virginia's high-quality coal to fire his fleet of locomotives."[2] This railroad mogul, who gave his name to one of the state's major cities, was not alone. John D. Rockefeller Sr. also acquired coal mining properties in both Paint Creek, West Virginia, and later in Colorado, profitable acquisitions which yielded lean and bloody outcomes for the miners of two states.[3]

Working at the behest of the coal companies, agents of Baldwin-Felts evicted the striking miners of Paint Creek from their company-owned houses. Those actions presented homeless miners with no refuge from the harsh elements other than moving their families into simple, canvas tents, supplied by the USWA. Despite the ravages of poverty and hunger, the indomitable miners and their families bravely soldiered on. Still unable to break the will of the strikers, agents shredded their tent colonies with machine gun fire, killing some of the less fortunate in their ranks. These brutal but effective atrocities were repeated in Colorado.

Huntington and Rockefeller were not alone in their acquisitions within the state. Others came to West Virginia as

1. David Corbin, "Life, Work, and Rebellion in the Coal Fields," (University of Illinois Press, 1981), p. 2.
2. Green, "The Devil is Here in These Hills," p. 17.
3. Ibid, p. 73.

well, hungering for the fortunes to be made from these almost endless, black resources. Often times, that required the wealthy and powerful to exploit or manipulate the legal system in order to acquire the lands over which these coal reserves were hidden, sometimes shoving aside the land's rightful owners in the process. "The state of West Virginia took possession of many old homesteads during the 1880s because the original settlers had not registered their deeds or paid taxes."[4] This blatant abuse created generations of bitter descendants in West Virginia, men like United Mine Workers District 17 President, Frank Keeney, whose ancestor, Moses Keeney, was one of the first ones to travel up the Kanawha River to make his home in the area of Eskdale in 1833.

Although coal was king in all of Appalachia, poverty reined in the coalfields of southern West Virginia in the latter part of the Nineteenth Century. Days were long; times were hard. Moreover, progress was earned slowly, if things ever truly changed at all. "The growth of the coal industry gave the coal operators a dominance in the state government over southern West Virginia until the New Deal."[5] This dominance was firmly exercised and regularly put on display for all to see in the company towns. "The coal companies built all their houses alike, usually A-frame, Jenny Lind-type, with the intention of housing the most people possible at the lowest cost...Outdoor water service was available to all miners free—only company officials had inside water. Outdoor privies in both sections were cleaned once a year without charge—only company officials had indoor toilets. The company provided free coal for fuel to all employees but charged fifty cents for delivery...The only store from which the miners could purchase their needs was the company store."[6] Many of those company towns only paid their miners in scrip, a form of coinage which could be utilized only in the company store. The few West Virginia coal companies which did pay their employees in cash would often blacklist, intimidate, or fire the miners who occasionally went outside their towns to acquire their food, clothing, and work implements.

There was nothing special about the birth of Charles E. Lively, another child thrust into the harsh economic conditions of southern West Virginia. But unlike most of those who entered this struggling environment, Charles wasn't destined to live out his life as only a coal miner, eking out a meager living for himself

---

4. Ibid, p. 17.
5. Corbin, "Life, Work, and Rebellion in the Coal Fields," p. 1.
6. Ibid, pp. 67, 68.

and his family from the black rock that he could dig from the heart of the earth. His was an unusual life, marked by controversy, deception, and numerous acts of extreme violence. In addition, several years of Charles' life were shrouded in great mystery.[7]

Born on March 6, 1887, in Spring Hill, West Virginia, this child of James Joseph Lively and Ameretta Parsons Lively became a central figure in the coal mine wars of two states, West Virginia and Colorado. In fact, his name was later associated with two of the most significant incidents of labor violence to ever take place in the United States of America, Ludlow and Matewan. Lively's actions were a precursor to the first event, and he soon became entangled to the aftermath of the latter. Of course, to his father and mother, Joseph and Ameretta, Charles was only a child, one of eleven. If they were similar to most parents, it's probable that this child was conceived in love, given birth in hope, and sent into the world with their wishes that he would enjoy a much better life than they had. However, not much can be documented about his parents, so one has to wonder about the influences Lively faced which ultimately drove him to adopt such a cloak-and-dagger lifestyle. Perhaps those influences instead came from something he saw, learned, or experienced from his older siblings, who often helped raise the children in large families. It is known that his parents suffered the tragic loss of a child, Amanda Lively, who was born and died on December 15, 1868, over twenty years before Charles entered the world.[8]

As a farmer, Joseph was forced to scratch out a tough living—planting and tending a few crops from the rocky West Virginia soil. At one point, it appears that he was forced to enter the mines to supplement what he earned from the farm. Ameretta, Charles' mother, was illiterate. At the age of thirteen, Charles had already attended school, long enough that he learned to both read and write. The 1900 federal census, which provides much of this information, also leaves the world with some other questions, such as how Charles E. Lively even came to be known

7. Thomas Felts' Papers, Eastern Regional Coal Archives, Bluefield, West Virginia. Absolutely nothing is known about Lively's undercover work in Illinois, except for his stubborn reluctance to talk about it under oath. "Unless that is absolutely necessary, I hate awful to divulge that place," Lively testified.
8. Lively Family records, Ancestry, www.ancestry.com.

by the moniker "Charles," at all. His father listed his son's name on the census as only, "Evert A."[9]

By the 1910 census, Charles E. Lively, a machine runner in a coal mine, resided in a boarding house in El Paso County in Colorado. He was then going by the name of "Everett Lively."[10] On his 1917 World War I draft registration, he was identified as "C. Everett Lively."[11] On the 1920 census, Lively's name was recorded as "Evert C."[12] Appearing on his World War II draft registration, he identified himself as "Charles Everett Lively."[13] Upon registering for Social Security, he selected the name of "Charles E. Lively."[14]

There is no clear or discernible explanation for when and why Lively's name, "Charles," first appeared. Perhaps that is one more secret that Lively carried to the grave. It is certainly reasonable to conclude, however, that Lively spent so much of his life as an undercover operative, he picked up the alias, Charles, somewhere during one of his assignments. Maybe the change in name became useful to Lively in preserving his anonymity. Perhaps some of the differed spellings may simply be attributed to the various educational backgrounds of those taking the census. It is clear, however, that the former Baldwin-Felts agent was generally using the name Charles Everett Lively, or those same initials, on nearly all official documents by 1940.

As a youth, Charles was friendly and persuasive, qualities which would eventually serve him well as an undercover agent. He soon developed a kinship with his pal, Fred Mooney, who later became a significant part of the leadership in United Mine Workers of America District 17. "Well, Mr. Mooney, he had known me," Charles stated, "ever since I was a boy, and known me at the time I first went into the union."[15] Both Charles and Mooney were well acquainted with the hardships of poverty since both their fathers were farmers who sought to earn a living from the rocky, West Virginia soil. "Had we not raised cows,

9. U.S. Census Bureau, 1900, Kanawha County, West Virginia, Conley Precinct, Ancestry, www.ancestry.com.
10. U.S. Census Bureau, 1910, El Paso County, Colorado, Precinct 54, Ancestry, www.ancestry.com.
11. World War I Draft Registration Cards, Ancestry, www.ancestry.com.
12. U.S. Census Bureau, 1920, Browns Creek District, West Virginia, Ancestry, www.ancestry.com.
13. World War I Draft Registration Cards, Ancestry, www.ancestry.com.
14. Social Security records, Ancestry, www.ancestry.com.
15. Ryan Hardesty, "Better World, Testimony to Congress on the Matewan Massacre-1921," The People of Matewan, (Homespun Press, 2018), p. 155.

pigs, and chickens, and farmed several acres of ground in corn, sorghum-cane, and garden truck," Fred Mooney wrote, "we would have been confronted by the wolf at the door many times."[16] Like many boys of the time, it can be speculated that whenever they could find time away from their daily chores, they explored the woods and hills. These childhood friends splashed, swam, and skipped rocks in Davis Creek.

Something else he had in common with his friend Charles, Mooney was also dissatisfied with their working environment and the dismal future consigned to them and their families, folks seemingly trapped in the depths of their company-owned, coalfield communities. Even as children, Charles and Mooney both approached the world hungrily, each of them seeking more for themselves than their hardscrabble peers. This pair of close-knit, boyhood friends eventually became the most bitter of enemies, because the UMWA, of which Mooney was a leader banned Lively from membership "for 99 years."[17] Moreover, an eerily similar and alarming fate awaited them in their final days on this earth.

Boyhood was but a brief, fleeting moment for Charles. Moreover, the responsibilities of adulthood came early for boys in the West Virginia coalfields. Coal mines and timber were generally the only means of employment for a young man in that part of the state. A day's wages for a man were seldom more than a dollar a day. A boy could expect to earn little more than twenty-five cents for a day's labor.

Charles was a young man in a big hurry. "I first started work in a coal mine," Lively said, "when I was about 13 years old."[18] Charles became a member of the United Mine Workers and received his first union card in 1902, in Blackband, West Virginia. Around the time of his middle teenage years, Charles obviously became dissatisfied with the mining wages or was just unwilling to accept his status as simply a coal miner. It was then he joined Baldwin-Felts.[19]

The Baldwin-Felts Detective Agency was initially started by William Gibboney Baldwin as Baldwin's Railroad Detectives. The agency provided security and police services to the Norfolk

---

16. Fred Mooney, "Struggle in the Coal Fields, The Autobiography of Fred Mooney," (West Virginia University Press, 1967), J.W. Hess, ed., p. 1.
17. Scott Martelle, "Blood Passion: The Ludlow Massacre and Class War in the American West," (Rutgers University Press, 2008), p. 56.
18. Ryan Hardesty, "Better World."
19. Ibid.

& Western Railroad coalfield region. In 1910, Baldwin changed the Agency's name to reflect the addition of his partner, Thomas Lafayette Felts, who used to work as one of his most trusted detectives. Felts had been a loyal and trusted agent, seriously wounded in 1900, while working as a detective for Baldwin in pursuit of murder suspect, William Lee. While being pursued, Lee shot Thomas Felts in the chest, the heavy .45 caliber slug just missed piercing the detective's heart.[20] Felts soon recovered and joined the agency as Vice President. The Baldwins, a precursor to Baldwin-Felts Detectives, made quite a name for themselves in law enforcement, with their successful efforts to pursue and capture suspects of the Allen family, who were involved in a brutal 1912 shooting at the Carroll County Court House in Hillsville, Virginia. After the verdict was handed down, the judge, a sheriff, and the prosecutor were all shot and killed. The court clerk and some of the jurors were wounded as well. Baldwin's agency and his young detective, Thomas L. Felts, successfully captured all those involved in the planning and execution of the attack. Like the Pinkerton Agency, Baldwin-Felts also offered their detective services to coal companies who wished to deter or quash any further unionization efforts from their miners. Moreover, it was in the pursuit of these activities when the name of the agency first became tainted. "This was a labor-baiting, strikebreaking organization," said former West Virginia Attorney General Howard Lee. "From 1909 to 1925 my law office was on the third floor and this Agency occupied the entire fourth floor of the same building. During that time, I became intimately acquainted with both Baldwin and Felts," who Lee called, "the two most feared and hated men in the mountains."[21]

"These guards were professional strikebreakers, all tried on a dozen industrial battlefields, and willing to shoot with or without provocation," the former state attorney general added. "They were led by Albert and Lee Felts, brothers of Thomas L. Felts, head of the agency."[22] To this day, there are those who wish to portray the detectives for Baldwin-Felts as nothing more than honest, hard-working lawmen. Others see them as little more than paid gunmen, heartless thugs, and indiscriminate killers. The truth obviously lies somewhere between those two extremes. There can certainly be no argument that, with

20. Velke, "The True Story of the Baldwin-Felts Detective Agency," pp. 42, 43.
21. Lee, "Bloodletting in Appalachia," pp 35, 53, 189, 190.
22. Ibid, p. 20.

Baldwin-Felts, numerous incidents of coalfield violence always followed in their wake. In the Report of the Commission on Industrial Relations, Mr. Luke Grant stated, "Espionage is closely related to violence. Sometimes it is the direct cause of violence, and where it cannot be charged, it is often the indirect cause."[23]

Unfortunately, the record does not clearly indicate if Baldwin-Felts first contacted Charles E. Lively or if he made the initial contact with them for employment. That fact remains under some dispute. The date largely corresponds with the beginnings of the miners' dissatisfaction over contractual issues with the coal operators in the Paint Creek and Cabin Creek regions of West Virginia, where numerous extreme acts of violence occurred, many of them attributed to the agents of Baldwin-Felts. One could conclude it is also quite likely that Lively heard the grumblings of his fellow miners and their desire to strike if conditions failed to improve. If this speculation holds true, perhaps he thought that this information would prove valuable to those entrusted with the protection of the mines.

William C. Blizzard, who grew up in the household of one of the union's most prominent leaders of that time, wrote this about Lively: "About 1912, when he was 24 years old, he was approached by a recruiter for the Baldwin-Felts Detective Agency."[24] According to the detective's sworn Senate testimony, Charles was asked when he first began doing "secret service" work for Baldwin-Felts, a term not to be confused with the United States Secret Service, which started in 1865, the same year Abraham Lincoln was assassinated.[25] Lively often referred to his undercover work for Baldwin-Felts as "secret service," the sound of which obviously appealed to the detective much more than the harsh realities of calling himself a labor spy. When the senators questioned him about his beginnings in labor espionage, "It was either in 1912 or 1913," Lively testified. "I was in Thurmond, W.Va."[26] However, the 1910 Federal Census indicates that Lively was already living in El Paso County, Colorado, and working in the nearby coal mines.

23. White, William, *The New Republic*, Volume 26, Republic Pub. Co, 1921, quoting Luke Grant.
24. William C. Blizzard, "Coal's Dramatic Period," *Charleston Gazette-Mail*, Charleston, West Virginia, June 16, 1963.
25. Hardesty, "A Better World," p. 126.
26. Ibid, p. 127. In the early twentieth century, Thurmond, WV, was a town of great corruption. Liquor, brothels, and gambling were rampant and murders were routine. The Dunglen Hotel had a running poker game there that never closed for years. In "Bloodletting in Appalachia," pp. 208-211. Howard Lee said, "It was said that one could get about anything he wanted at the Dunglen

Since poverty was rampant in the coal mining communities of West Virginia, it seems unlikely that a miner's paltry wages would allow Charles, or nearly any miner—particularly the son of a poor, West Virginia farmer—the luxury to venture from West Virginia to Colorado on a whim. Therefore, it isn't unreasonable to speculate that Charles also began drawing a second income from Baldwin-Felts almost two full years before his testimony claimed. Immediately upon his arrival in Colorado, Lively procured employment with Pike View mine, of the Pikes Peak Coal Company. It was at this time when Charles E. Lively first revealed his extraordinary ability to survive through difficult circumstances, almost as if he had nine lives. *The Colorado Springs Gazette* reported that Everett (one similar report also wrongly lists his name as Ernest) Lively was injured "yesterday morning, 15 minutes after he secured employment."[27]

It can, however, be speculated that the newspaper's use of the name, "Ernest," may have been more than a simple discrepancy in reporting. Perhaps it was a deliberate attempt to hide Lively's identity, by using an alias, something the undercover detective later employed when he was arrested for crimes in West Virginia. If Charles E. Lively was already going by an alias in Colorado, it would add credibility to the notion that he was already doing secret service work for Baldwin-Felts in 1910, almost two full years before his sworn testimony indicated. Or perhaps this mine fall incident may have been the moment where his contact with Baldwin-Felts was first made.

The newspaper also stated, "...Lively, 23 years old, narrowly escaped death. He was caught beneath a slab of coal seven feet long and weighing almost a ton, but escaped with a few bruises. Lively was taken to St. Francis Hospital. He came here from West Virginia a few days ago." One of the early *Gazette* headlines, "Lively Cannot Live," reported that Charles was so badly crushed in the mine disaster, he wasn't expected to survive. Reading further, the report additionally stated that "he cannot live more than two or three days."[28] Obviously, the reports of the detective's eminent death were greatly exaggerated. Charles E. Lively not only survived this 1910 Colorado, coal mining disaster; he thrived.

---

or any other place in town." It is therefore not surprising that Thurmond was the place in which Charles E. Lively first made contact with the Baldwin-Felts agency.

27. *Colorado Springs Gazette*, Colorado Springs, Colorado, January 28, 1910, and February 5, 1910.
28. Ibid.

Baldwin-Felts badges, displayed at the Baldwin House in Bluefield, West Virginia.

(JoEllen Yoho)

Southern West Virginia

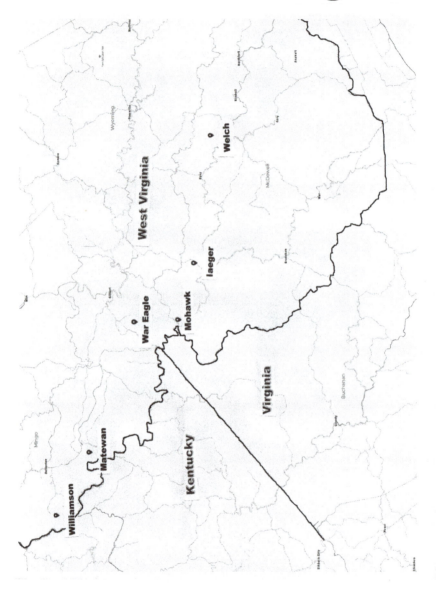

Much of Charles Everett Lively's work for the Baldwin-Felts Detective Agency took place in the towns detailed on this map.

(Map by J. Keith Jones)

CHAPTER 3
Early Work in West Virginia

According to his own testimony, Charles E. Lively first came to Matewan, West Virginia, in "about 1910 or 11." It isn't clear what Lively did while he was briefly in the South, but Lively said, "I just returned from the state of Florida, where I had spent a winter." Lively continued, "I talked to John Walker, Manager of the Selden Machinery Company in Huntington about a job, and he sent me up there to see about running the machine, but I didn't stay at that time." According to Lively, on this, his first visit to Matewan, he stayed "just a couple of days" and "didn't go to work."[1] But Lively's detective work for Baldwin-Felts eventually returned him to Matewan, his next appearance in the town being something which the locals could never forget, or forgive.

On July 1, 1911, Charles was married to Icie Bell Goff, the daughter of Joe Goff and Mary Painter, in Charleston, West Virginia. He was twenty-four years old at the time; Icie was twenty-one. Theirs wasn't always a happy union. Time progressed, years passed, and Lively's extended undercover work out west separated the couple, adding to the rising tension between them.

Although the two of them remained married throughout their lives, the record also indicates that Charles was anything but faithful in the vows he took to his wife. Some evidence suggests Lively, in addition to womanizing, was also abusive toward his wife and children. In fact, unfaithfulness and casual disregard for the vows and oaths that Lively often swore to uphold proved to be the greatest hallmark of the agent's life and career. Despite their apparent difficulties and his time spent away from the family, Charles and his wife, Icie, were quite fruitful when it came to the matter of offspring. Their union produced nine children: Lillian, Everett, Arnold, Charles Albert, Gordon, Gladys, Russell, Marjorie, and Paul.[2]

---

1. Testimony at the Matewan defendants' murder trial in Williamson, West Virginia, 1921.
2. Icie B. Lively Obituary, Newspaper Archive, www.newspaperarchive.com, July 18, 2018. There are conflicting documents regarding number of children.

Once Charles E. Lively was fully engaged as a spy with Baldwin-Felts, his travels routinely brought him back and forth between West Virginia and his other assignments in the west. All the while, his reputation and value to the agency was growing. While working, as Lively called it, 'secret service,' for the agency, he behaved in all the ways he earnestly believed a loyal union man might conduct himself. Lively described it as "making myself an active member."[3] He won the confidence of the miners and obviously accomplished those objectives, since nobody apparently questioned his loyalty to the United Mine Workers, District 17.

While coal reigned in southern West Virginia, the profession was a tough and dangerous means of employment. The coal mining communities gave birth to some daring and hardy souls. Corruption was rampant in the coalfields. In their desire to seek some relief from coal company abuses—intimidation, violence, blacklists—the miners risked everything to join a union. This was indeed the perfect environment for a charming deceiver like Charles E. Lively to infiltrate their ranks. "Lively was described as a medium-sized, stocky man with a pleasant smile. According to one reporter who knew him, 'He showed unmistakable signs of a winning personality; it was easy to imagine him gaining the confidence of any group of workmen.'"[4]

Early in his undercover career for Baldwin-Felts, Lively was a delegate to a miners' convention which took place in Charleston, West Virginia, for District 29. He was representing the Gatewood Local in the New River field. "The miners paid my expenses there to that Charleston convention; yes," Lively said, "I felt that it was necessary that I leave them [the union] pay them [Lively's expenses] in order to keep off suspicion, or else they would wonder why I would not want them [the union] to pay them [his expenses]."[5]

Around the time Lively first joined Baldwin-Felts, West Virginia experienced massive labor unrest in both the Paint Creek and Cabin Creek regions of the state. Miners were striking for higher wages, better working conditions, and accurate measurements of the coal cars they loaded, while the southern West Virginia coal operators were cracking down on their efforts to unionize their regions. For these efforts, coal companies often blacklisted strikers from digging coal in other nearby mines.

3. Hardesty, "Better World," p. 146.
4. Velke, "The True Story of the Baldwin-Felts Detective Agency," p. 176.
5. Hardesty, "Better World," p. 132.

Some strikers were evicted from their company owned homes and forced to move into tent colonies provided by the union. Martial law was declared when numerous acts of violence occurred, not all of them attributable to the striking miners. Those declarations of martial law did nothing to alter the behavior of the coal company executives; however, they greatly limited the activities and freedom of the striking miners and their families.

"There has never been an exact count for the West Virginia Mine Wars, but the conflict left its dead across the southern counties. One of the best-known cases is that of Francis F. "Cesco" Estep, the victim of the infamous 'Bull Moose Special' raid on a tent colony set up by striking miners at Holly Grove on Paint Creek. The darkened special, an armored train built by the coal operators for the purpose of transporting scabs and mine guards, crept through Holly Grove on the night of February 7, 1913, pouring machine gun fire into the tents and houses of the community. Miraculously, Estep was the only fatality, falling dead at the feet of his pregnant wife."[6]

By casting his lot with Baldwin-Felts during this troubled time, Lively joined one of the most hated organizations in the state. In fact, it is doubtful that he could have chosen a more dangerous or despised form of employment for the era in which he lived. "The Baldwin-Felts men were also spies and snoopers, who for years had built up files of the names of Union men which went to all operators," according to William C. Blizzard. "If you opened your mouth to talk Union in West Virginia you were not only fired but you couldn't get a job in the mines anywhere in the state."[7]

The information supplied by Baldwin-Felts agents on the identities of miners joining the union, and the names of the organizers who recruited them, resulted in the firing, blacklisting, evicting, beating, and sometimes even the death of those individuals. The agents operated in secrecy throughout the coal camps, often posing as faithful union men, loyal to the struggles faced by the miners. During later Senate testimony, Lively seemingly failed to understand and appeared oblivious to the utter contempt directed his way from Senator Kenneth

6. Lois McLean, "Blood Flows on the Creeks, The Killing of Estep and Woodrum," Ken Sullivan, ed., "The Goldenseal Book of the West Virginia Mine Wars," (Quarrier Press, 1991), p. 48.
7. William C. Blizzard, Wess Harris, ed., "When Miners March," (PM Press, 2010), p. 68.

McKellar, a Democrat from Tennessee. While upon the stand, Lively, the Baldwin-Felts operative, testified about his double life and how he routinely betrayed his oath to uphold the union.

"Do you think," Sen. McKellar asked, "that was the right action on your part."

"Yes," Lively said.

McKellar continued, "And you cannot see anything wrong in that action?"

"I do not."

McKellar was staggered by the detective's sensibilities regarding right and wrong. "And you think it is entirely right and justifiable?"

"I do," Lively responded.[8]

The detective was obviously tone-deaf to the senator's sense of moral outrage, and despite Lively's strong defense as to the rectitude of his actions, McKellar was unconvinced.

"I will say that it violated every idea of right that I ever had," Sen McKellar said. "I never would have believed that a thing like this would happen, and I am not surprised that you are having trouble down there in Mingo County."[9]

But the troubles in Mingo County weren't about to go away anytime soon. In fact, the hardships for the region were just beginning. According to author, David Corbin: "By sealing off the area to UMWA organizers, the Baldwin-Felts guards insured that any uprising of the southern West Virginia coal diggers would begin with the miners themselves and guaranteed that the union spirit that evolved in southern West Virginia—and that the ideas and ideals the miners formulated about unionism and about what unionism should represent—would reflect the character and values of the rank-and-file miners, not the international union."[10]

Despite his obvious lack of conscience, Lively did, however, fully understand the risks he faced as an undercover operative for Baldwin-Felts. Living a double life and trying to keep those two, contrasting lives separate must have been a daunting task. Not only did Lively fill out expense accounts to be sent back to his local union regarding his organizing activities, he was also required to prepare regular expense accounts and intelligence

8. Hardesty, "Better World,", p. 137.
9. Ibid, pp. 136-141.
10. Corbin, "Life Work, and Rebellion in the Coal Fields," p. 52.

reports, which he forwarded to his superiors at Baldwin-Felts. Lively was like a man walking a tightrope without a net; there was little margin for error. Mailing those expense accounts to the wrong place, putting down a wrong name, or any such mistake could have resulted in his secret life being exposed. A single slip-up could have led to Lively being killed. The detective not only led multiple lives; the record indicates that there were times those conflicting lives encroached upon one another.

"If you had disclosed your connection with the detective agency," Sen. McKellar asked, "do you suppose the miners would have let you in there at all?"

"I think," Lively stated, "they would have turned me over to the undertaker."[11]

As Charles E. Lively testified before those numerous Senators in Washington, he exhibited no shame, no guilt, and also, no fear. In those dark, undercover years of his life with Baldwin-Felts, the detective knew any misstep could get him killed. Moreover, the dangers Lively faced while living those many years behind his mask might have proven to be a strain on most men; yet there is no evidence that Lively found this life as anything other than exhilarating. He loved being an agent. Perhaps the only thing Charles E. Lively truly feared was a life without his detective work for Baldwin-Felts.

---

11. Hardesty, "Better World," p. 135.

Huerfano County Sheriff Jeff Farr.
(Huerfano County Historical Association)

CHAPTER 4
Colorado Corruption
and the Ludlow Massacre

After leaving West Virginia, Charles E. Lively's work for Baldwin-Felts took him far across the country, to places where he often plied his trade as both a miner and a detective. "The opportunity to provide secret service men and detectives in the western coalfields did not escape the attention of Thomas Felts," wrote John A. Velke in his book, *The True Story of the Baldwin-Felts Detective Agency*. "The Agency soon established an office in Denver, Colorado, and installed Albert Felts as the manager."[1] Sometime after 1910, Lively became affiliated with the Western Federation of Miners, where he worked as a union organizer and became their president, for which he also drew a salary.[2]

Albert Felts sent Lively to Huerfano County, Colorado, the Spanish Peaks region of the state, a place once roamed by the Apache and Comanche, known as "Huajatolla," or "Breasts of the World." The Indians believed these breasts to the south gave nourishment to huerfano, Spanish for "the Orphan," from which the county took its name, a dark lonely, volcanic butte, rising over 200 feet above the plains. The Utes feared the Spanish Peaks region, believing it to be the dwelling place of evil spirits and angry gods. Spanish conquistadors are rumored to have found gold there and French trappers discovered another kind of wealth nearby in the fur trade. Explorers and settlers used those peaks as a reliable set of navigational landmarks. The region was later described as follows: "Explorers, lawmen, gunslingers, and mountain men with names like Kit Carson, Black Jack Ketchum, Wild Bill Hickock, John C. Fremont, Uncle Dick Wootton, Zane Grey, William Bent, and Bat Masterson frequently traveled the area."[3] It was populated by the Spanish, followed later by German settlers, each of them leaving some stamp of their own distinctive cultures upon the area. The Spanish Peaks eventually became famous for the vast deposits of coal to be mined there,

1. Velke, "The True Story of the Baldwin-Felts Detective Agency," p. 175.
2. Hardesty, "Better World," pp. 137, 155.
3. "A People's History of the Spanish Peaks," www.SpanishPeaksCountry.com, July 19, 2019.

and infamous for the actions of those who profited from the mines.

While in Colorado, Lively was ordered to infiltrate the La Veta local while "working on a murder case"[4] for the agency. Gregarious, persuasive, and still going by the name of Everett Lively, the detective was not only successful in his mission; he was also falsely perceived to be a good and loyal union man, which led to him being elected vice president of his local union in La Veta. Lively's investigation there was responsible for finding evidence which led to the murder arrest of John Flockheart, who was the secretary of that same La Veta local.

"I was sent out there to investigate a case where the United Mine Workers or the union men had shot and killed some men that passed the road in automobiles, and I think that four were killed and one was wounded, and that they left two dead," Lively testified. "My investigation led to the getting of a lot of evidence that had not been gotten and the locating and apprehending of one man that was implicated in that murder. I found on investigation that he had furnished some of the rifles and had planned it and told the place to go to do it; that he had some of the rifles planted in his yard and went out and dug them up and gave them to these men. He was arrested near Rock Springs, WY, and brought back."[5]

Lively's next assignment took him to Walsenburg, which is approximately fifteen miles northeast from the town of La Veta. Before he went to Walsenburg, Lively had one final duty to perform for Baldwin-Felts in La Veta. It was a mission that would instantly establish Lively's reputation as a dedicated, loyal, and deadly agent. At the turn of the century, Walsenburg was a booming, Colorado community on the edge of nowhere. With its two newspapers and six churches, Walsenburg resided at the crossroads of our nation's legendary Old West and America's blossoming industrial age. Those two worlds ultimately collided in Walsenburg, and coal was key to the area's remarkable growth.

In the ten years following the 1900 Census, Walsenburg and its nearby city, La Veta, saw their towns double in population. According to *A History of the Colorado Coal Field War*, "Most of the miners lived in these canyons in company towns, in company houses, bought food and equipment at company stores and alcohol at company saloons. The doctors, priests, schoolteachers,

4. Hardesty, "Better World," p.140
5. Ibid, pp. 141, 142.

Sheriff Jeff Farr, on horseback, far left of picture.
(*Huerfano County Historical Association*)

and law enforcement were all company employees."[6] Despite the work to be readily gained by strong and willing hands—and the rapid growth experienced by these communities—many of the miners were unsatisfied with the dangerous working conditions. "The Colorado mines themselves were notoriously unsafe, among the most dangerous in the nation, second only to Utah. Miners died in Colorado coal mines at over twice the national average."[7]

Along with the numerous coal mining camps in the region, Walsenburg was also home to one of the most corrupt sheriffs in the state's history. "The Walsenburg power structure was ruled by its sheriff, Jefferson B. Farr, who was whole-heartedly the tool of the coal industry. He was known far and wide as 'The King of Huerfano County' or 'Czar Farr.' As the coal mining industry grew, the need to control the miners also grew, and Jeff Farr was just the man to handle the job."[8] But it was his younger brother, Ed, who first became the sheriff of Huerfano County. Ed employed Jeff as one of his deputies. "Jeff Farr was one of three sons who left their native Texas to become the biggest

6. "A History of the Colorado Coal Field War," Colorado Coal Field War Project, University of Denver, www.du.edu/ludlow/, August 21, 2019.
7. Ibid.
8. Dorothy Ree, "Walsenburg - Crossroads Town," (Nocturne Independent Publishing, 2006), p. 58.

cattle dealers in southern Colorado."[9] Jeff, Ed, and Dave Farr
dominated the county's politics for many years. Jeff and Ed Farr
were primarily lawmen; their brother, Dave, sometimes served as
an undersheriff. He was basically a hanger-on, a political
opportunist who basked in the notoriety and power of his two
better-known brothers. "During the course of three successive
terms the political machine Farr created ran elections and law
courts for the benefit of the Party and the Colorado Fuel and
Iron Company," wrote Senator George McGovern in his book,
The Great Coalfield War. "To his cattle interests he added real
estate and wholesale liquor, thereby gaining control of saloons
and brothels. A prominent citizen of Walsenburg whose sheer
survival as a critic of the Farr machine owed much to his
advanced age and distinguished Civil War service charged that
virtually all of the county's forty-five saloons belonged to the
Spanish Peaks Mercantile Company of which Jeff Farr was
president."[10]

Ed and Jeff were a pair of lawmen with vastly different
approaches to upholding the law. Ed Farr was an Old West-style
lawman. A Texan by birth, he ruled by the six-gun, doing battle
with cattle rustlers and numerous border bandits. Ed was
subsequently murdered in 1899, in Turkey Creek Canyon, near
Cimarron, in the New Mexico Territory, while his posse was
pursuing a gang of outlaws. "At the height of their prosperity,"
Sen. McGovern wrote. "Edwin Farr was elected sheriff of
Huerfano County and was into his second term," when he was
struck down.[11] The outlaw gang, led by Thomas "Black Jack"
Ketchum, "held up the Colorado & Southern passenger train at
Folsom..." the *Helena Weekly Independent* reported. "Sheriff Ed
Farr received the first wound through the wrist, but bandaged it
and resumed the battle. He was shot a second time through the
body and fell dead."[12]

Black Jack Ketchum continued his streak of lawlessness for
most of the next two years. In April 1901, the law finally caught
up with the bandit and he was sent to the gallows in Clayton,
New Mexico Territory. The hangman failed to do his job
properly and Ketchum's head was removed by the noose. After
pulling the blind over his head, Ketchum uttered, "Goodbye,"

9. George McGovern, Leonard Guttridge, "The Great Coalfield War,"
    (Houghton Mifflin, 1972), p. 31.
10. Ibid, p. 32.
11. Ibid, p. 31.
12. *Helena Weekly Independent*, Helena, MT, July 20, 1899.

and the trap was sprung. "When the body dropped through the trap the half-inch rope severed his head as cleanly as if a knife had cut it," the *Phoenix Arizona Republican* wrote. "The body pitched forward, with blood spurting from the headless trunk. The head remained in the black sack and flew down into the pit. Some men groaned and others turned away, unable to endure the sight."[13]

Upon Ed Farr's death, Jefferson Farr, his deputy, took over his position as the county sheriff. But unlike his older brother, Jeff Farr didn't rule by the six-gun. His weapon of choice was politics, commanding such a powerful county machine of electoral and judicial dominance that few would dare to successfully challenge him. "Jefferson Farr succeeded his late brother as sheriff, swearing vengeance against evildoers, and as his subsequent career made plain, these he was quick to identify as union organizers, labor agitators, and all foes of the county Republican Party," Sen. McGovern wrote.[14]

In another departure from his late brother's approach, Jeff Farr also wasn't willing to endanger his life in the commission of his law enforcement duties, once refusing to protect an accused prisoner from an angry mob of vigilantes. A black, Pullman Car porter, W.H. Wallace, was accused of ravishing "an aged lady who arrived last night from Los Angeles," according to the *Jacksonville Daily Illinois Courier*.[15] Although the sheriff made some feeble efforts to get Wallace out of town and away from danger, Farr readily surrendered the accused man to the rowdy band of armed vigilantes who pursued them. After snatching the accused railroad porter from the sheriff, the mob later lynched Wallace upon a nearby telegraph pole and repeatedly shot holes into his body with their pistols. The news story stated: "Sheriff Farr made no resistance."[16] With one soul taken and his own life spared, Jeff Farr, owing his power to the aid of the coal companies, continued tightening his grip on Huerfano County and on the town of Walsenburg. Farr was a corporate sheriff, owing much of his local dominance and political clout to the powerful Colorado Fuel and Iron Company. "Farr's interests," Sen. McGovern wrote in his book, "were indistinguishable from those of the CFI."[17] It must also be stated that even the salaries of

13. *Phoenix Arizona Republican*, Phoenix, Arizona, April 27, 1901.
14. McGovern, "The Great Coalfield War," p. 31.
15. *Jacksonville Daily Illinois Courier*, Jacksonville, IL. March 26, 1902.
16. Ibid.
17. McGovern, "The Great Coalfield War," p. 31.

Huerfano County Courthouse, Walsenburg, Colorado, which is still standing today. The Huerfano County Jail is behind the courthouse, to the left.

(Huerfano County Historical Association)

Huerfano County Jail, as it looks today. The building currently serves as the Walsenburg Mining Museum.

(Huerfano County Historical Association)

Above the front of the front door of the Walsenburg [Colorado] Mining Museum.

(Author's collection)

Period map of Huerfano County, Colorado.

(Huerfano County Historical Association)

most of Sheriff Farr's deputies came directly from the company coffers.[18]

In her book, *Walsenburg - Crossroads Town*, Dorothy Ree penned the following observations: "In due time the old Colorado Coal and Iron Co. became the Colorado Fuel and Iron Co. Its principal stockholder was John D. Rockefeller, Sr., and the property was supposed to be under the supervision of John D. Rockefeller, Jr. The mines were under the direct supervision of managers and executives like Jesse Welborn and LaMont Montgomery Bowers, who reported on conditions to Rockefeller at his New York Office. Their reports invariably said that the miners were all happy in their work situation and with their wages. All labor unrest was attributed to the efforts of the United Mine Workers to organize the workers. Rockefeller trusted his coal mine operators implicitly. He had never visited his western properties and saw no reason to do so. The word of his management team that all was well and that the miners were satisfied workers was enough for him."[19]

But like the strikers in West Virginia, the coal miners in the Spanish Peaks region were angered with their working conditions. Besides the numerous safety hazards faced by the miners, the economic conditions were appalling. "Miners were required to buy their own tools, boots, black powder and anything else they might need," according to Dorothy Ree's book. "The miner was in debt to the company store before he ever set foot inside the mine and he rarely, if ever, was able to get out of that debt. That labor unrest was a part of the mining scene in Huerfano County almost from the moment the first mine was opened was undeniable."[20]

Testimony before a federal commission on industrial relations revealed the abysmal state of political corruption in Walsenburg in general and by Jefferson Farr in particular. Before that commission in December 1914, Joseph Patterson testified: "There is no form of government in Huerfano County. They call it the Kingdom of Farr. It has been declared by the majority of people down there to be not a part of Colorado; but they call it the Kingdom of Farr, through the influence of Colorado Fuel & Iron Co.; we don't recognize it as part of the United States."[21] In further testimony regarding the sheriff, a witness said, "He was

18. *Nevada State Journal*, Reno, Nevada, December 10, 1914.
19. Ree, "Walsenburg, Crossroads Town," p. 64.
20. Ibid, p. 61.
21. "Hellraisers Journal: They Call it the Kingdom of Jefferson Farr, Through the Influence of the CF&I Company," *The Daily Kos*,

in the wholesale liquor business, supplying all but about ten of the forty-four saloons in the country, twenty-two of them in Walsenburg."[22] Another witness stated, "Saloon people who do not buy off him frequently find their places closed as disorderly houses."[23]

In addition to the rampant political corruption in the Colorado coal camps, violations of mine safety practices and instances of miner deaths were rarely, if ever, found to be the fault of the companies. "Hand-picked coroner's juries absolved the coal companies of responsibility almost without exception," stated in *A History of the Colorado Coal Field War.* "For example, in the years from 1904-1914, the juries picked by the Sheriff of Huerfano County, Jeff Farr, found the coal operators to blame in only one case out of 95."[24]

In *Walsenburg – Crossroads Town*, Dorothy Ree wrote: "Jeff Farr continued his harassment of striking miners and other citizens whose sympathies lay with the workers. His deputies showed great brutality towards the strikers."[25] Striking workers were often beaten and arrested. They were evicted from company-owned houses and dwelt in cold and meager tents. Clashes broke out between strikers and Farr's deputies, which resulted in some of the strikers being shot to death. Even Mary Harris "Mother" Jones, who traveled the country as an advocate for striking miners, was arrested at the Walsenburg train station and imprisoned at the Huerfano County Jail.[26]

It was also learned, in preparation for the upcoming coal strike of September 23, 1913, that Farr hired over three hundred and twenty-six deputies the first nine months of the year, without any regard or questions as to their qualifications or backgrounds. "Included in this number," John Velke wrote, "were Albert Felts and several other Baldwin-Felts agents."[27] It was reported by the *Joplin Globe* that these individuals merely had to request work and were hired "as deputy sheriffs at the

https://www.dailykos.com/stories/2014/12/11/1350811/-Hellraisers-Journal-They-call-it-the-Kingdom-of-Farr-through-the-influence-of-the-CF-I-Company, January 7, 2020.
22. *Nevada State Journal*, Reno, NV, December 10, 1914.
23. *Fort Wayne Journal Gazette*, Fort Wayne, Indiana, December 8, 1914.
24. *A History of the Colorado Coal Field War*, Colorado Coal Field War Project.
25. Ree, "Walsenburg, Crossroads Town," p. 69.
26. "Steeped in History," "City of Walsenburg—A Great Place to Be," November 10, 2019.
27. Velke, John, "The True Story of the Baldwin-Felts Detective Agency," p. 175.

request of E.F. Matteson, division superintendent of the Colorado Fuel and Iron Company. These men were armed and paid by the company."[28] With no regard to this ever-growing list of illegalities and ethical improprieties, Sheriff Farr was content to do as his benefactors at Colorado Fuel and Iron suggested.

"So far as you know then," asked Mr. Walsh, chairman of the commission, "a red-handed murderer might have been among them and been given a commission?"

"So far as I know," replied the sheriff."[29]

As the strike continued, tensions grew in the Colorado coalfields, of which there were dozens of mines around the Spanish Peaks region. The violence soon escalated as well; murderous and bloodthirsty acts which were perpetrated from each side of the conflict. Deputies committed acts of violence on the strikers and the strikers retaliated by taking up arms to shoot the mine guards, some of whom were agents of Baldwin-Felts. Claiming that his agents were simply the innocent victims of the strikers' random acts of violence, Albert Felts took special precautions to protect his men. Felts testified "the armored auto the guards used was equipped with a steel body at the Pueblo plant of the Colorado Fuel & Iron Co., and then shipped to Trinidad. He [Albert Felts] admitted the machine gun mounted on it was shipped from West Virginia where the mine guards had used it in a strike last year. He said the operators paid the transportation on the gun."[30]

"He [Albert Felts] designed the first 'armored car,' nicknamed the 'Death Special' by the miners. He equipped the vehicle with a Colt machine gun capable of firing 33 rounds in five seconds. The gun was mounted on a tripod pedestal, which gave it the ability to pan 360 degrees and tilt up and down."[31] The Baldwin-Felts Agency contended this weapon was employed only for defensive purposes. "Later, Tom Felts would claim that if there were machine guns used in the Colorado strike violence, they did not belong to the Baldwin-Felts agency and he knew nothing about who might have fired them. He had made the same denial about the machine guns used against union miners in the Paint Creek-Cabin Creek strike in West Virginia."[32] In fact, that region of West Virginia was so deadly, Governor William

28. *Joplin Globe*, Joplin, Missouri, December 10, 1914.
29. Ibid.
30. *Montrose Daily Press*, Montrose, Colorado, February 12, 1914.
31. Velke, "The True Story of the Baldwin-Felts Detective Agency," p. 179.
32. Shogan, "The Battle of Blair Mountain," p. 18.

Glasscock's Adjutant General, Major Charles D. Elliott once said, "God does not walk these hills."[33]

Both miners and detectives in Colorado were shot and killed in the course of the conflict. Neither side had hands that were totally unstained by these senseless acts of bloodshed. In one notable incident, Sheriff Farr's "trigger-happy" deputies opened fire and killed three striking miners. Fearing retribution and gunplay from the outraged miners, the deputies fled to the strength and safety of the local courthouse, waiting there for help to arrive. Farr contacted a nearby sheriff and asked him to send help. The Las Animas County Sheriff dispatched ten of his deputies. Albert Felts traveled with them to Walsenburg, bringing about a peaceful resolution to a potentially explosive situation.[34]

As a result of the importation of hundreds of deputized officers, most of whom were men of dubious and uncertain reputations who strictly owed their allegiance to the coal companies, conditions only got worse for the strikers and their families. In the case of miners near Trinidad, "Mayor Dunleavy called upon the chief of police to furnish protection to thirty-five miners reported discharged from the Delaqua mine, seven miles from Ludlow. The men, who say they were driven from the camp at the point of guns and herded for five hours in Ludlow station, took refuge in the miners' headquarters, which was immediately surrounded by Baldwin-Felts detectives.[35]

Armed Baldwin-Felts agents evicted the southern Colorado strikers from their company-owned houses in much the same manner they employed earlier in the Paint Creek and Cabin Creek region of West Virginia, not many years before. "And then the grim struggle of the coal miners in Colorado jumped into the headlines. 'Hell and Repeat,'" that's what the miners called the West Virginia and Colorado strikes. And hell they were," wrote William C. Blizzard in the book, *When Miners March*.[36] More evicted miners were forced to move into tent colonies, such as those around Ludlow. The tents were provided for them by the UMWA, accommodations which were barely sufficient to protect the miners' families from the ravaging snow, sub-zero temperatures, and bitter winds of Colorado, perhaps weather

33. Green, James, "The Devil is Here in These Hills," 96.
34. Velke, "The True Story of the Baldwin-Felts Detective Agency," p. 179, 180.
35. *Del Norte San Juan Prospector*, Del Norte, Colorado, September 6, 1913.
36. Blizzard, "When Miners March," p. 101.

much worse than anything faced by striking miners in West Virginia.

The tents offered scant protection from other threats as well. "And the militia and guards were more murderous than in West Virginia. You might say that the West Virginia strike was a sort of 'boot camp' in which thugs, detectives, state officials, and coal operators received their training for the Colorado wars."[37] There were numerous incidents of machine gun fire being directed into the miners' tents, causing many of the approximately 1,100 miners and their families to dig pits underneath them and cover the holes over with lumber. It offered the wives and children a makeshift place of shelter and nearby escape when the bullets started shredding the thin layers of canvas which surrounded them. As the bloodletting grew more commonplace, both sides called for Governor Elias Ammons to send in the Colorado National Guard to quell the violence. The violence continued and a small contingent of troops were ordered into the area, while the governor sought to negotiate a settlement.

When Governor Ammons' efforts to reach a peaceful end proved to be fruitless, the state militia added reinforcements and martial law was declared. The striking miners believed the troops would offer them an added measure of protection; the coal operators saw the Guardsmen as a means to pass along the expenses of securing their mines and equipment to the state. In testimony to the commission, Reverend Henry Atkinson stated, "It soon became evident that the militia was under the control of the coal companies." He continued, "The militia instead of aiming to maintain order and secure justice was used to break the strike."[38] In March, Governor Ammons falsely believed the worst of the crisis was over. He withdrew a majority of the troops, leaving only a small detachment under the brutal leadership of Lieutenant Karl Linderfelt, "who enjoyed roughing up strikers and taunting them with racial and ethical slurs."[39]

"Not all militiamen were hostile to the strikers. Members of both groups belonged to the union-friendly Freemasons, which worked behind the scenes to maintain a fragile peace. But the units that were friendliest to the strikers were withdrawn by April 17, leaving a 200-man force, dominated by mine guards. Most vicious commander of the residual force was Lt. Karl

---

37. Ibid, P. 102
38. *Jacksonville Daily Journal*, Jacksonville, Illinois, November 24, 1914
39. *Colorado Springs Gazette-Telegraph*, Colorado Springs, Colorado, April 24, 1994.

Linderfelt," according to the *Colorado Springs Gazette-Telegraph*. "Linderfelt was a mean-spirited man with some limited military experience," the newspaper continued, "who was later convicted for assault on a Colorado striker, Louis Tikas, who he bashed in the head with the butt of his rifle. After the incident, Tikas was found dead, shot three times in the back, leaving most observers to believe he was also murdered at the same time by the lieutenant.[40]

About the time martial law was declared, Baldwin-Felts sought to remove most of their agents from these areas of conflict. The agency's manager, Albert Felts, chose to remain behind. Also not seeking to extricate himself from the growing hostilities in Colorado was the steadfastly loyal operative, Charles E. Lively. There were still undercover duties which the detective could successfully accomplish. Thanks to Jeff Farr's close connections to the coal owners, and at the behest of Albert Felts, Charles E. Lively performed some of his darkest and most sinister undercover work for Baldwin-Felts. In order to fulfill his mission, Lively needed to get into the Huerfano County Jail for an extended period of time. And what better way is there to get into jail quickly than by committing a murder? While still living in La Veta, the detective went to Pete Lage's Saloon in search of a victim. Or perhaps he went to the saloon with a specific victim in mind.

Not much is truly known about Swanson Oleen. He was born in Sweden in 1859, only four years before West Virginia officially became a state. Longing to earn a better life for himself, Oleen crossed a vast ocean to find work in the United States in 1885. Work was plenteous in the Colorado coalfields when Oleen settled there, joining many of those who migrated to the States around the turn of the century. "The workforce itself was largely immigrant labor from Southern and Eastern Europe," according to *A History of the Colorado Coal Field War*, "who had been brought in as strikebreakers in 1903."[41]

According to the 1900 Federal Census, Swan Oleen and his wife, Ida, lived in Pueblo, Colorado, with their two children. Swan was forty and Ida was twenty-eight. In the time leading up to the census, Swan Oleen had been without work for almost six months. At some point in their marriage, Ida became dissatisfied with their life together and divorced him in 1909, taking his two

40. Ibid.
41. *A History of the Colorado Coal Field War*, Colorado Coal Field War Project.

daughters, leaving Swan alone. After his divorce, Oleen continued to work in the Colorado coal mines but eventually joined the growing contingent of strikers.[42]

Like many of those seeking to wash away their troubles at the end of a long day, Swan Oleen walked into the saloon, an establishment owned by Pete Lage, an Italian immigrant. The date was April 11, 1914. Swan had no reason to believe his weekend would be different from any other, but it ultimately proved to be his final Saturday night upon the earth.

Sometime after entering the saloon, Oleen became engaged in a harsh, verbal dispute with Charles E. Lively. To witnesses inside the saloon, it appeared that Oleen was the aggressor from the outset and that Lively sought to avoid the confrontation. But Lively was already an expert at misleading others. The altercation continued, eventually growing to the point where Lively grabbed for his pistol and shot the striking miner, a wound that proved to be fatal. Lively later testified, "I shot a man in self-defense in order to save my own life."[43] But even though he told the Senate hearing that he killed Oleen in self-defense, none of the witnesses or accompanying news reports ever said anything about the other man being armed. In the course of the shooting, Oleen was seriously wounded and taken to the Minnequa hospital, where he died at seven o'clock the following Monday morning.[44]

"When it was over with," Lively testified, "I went up to the State militia, the lieutenant's, went up to his house to surrender, to give myself up and was taken to jail, and it was confided in the sheriff who I was—and a little later the State's attorney general—and I stayed there in jail not wanting a trial."[45] With Lively's unquestioned dedication and loyalty to Baldwin-Felts, it is doubtful that Swan Oleen was simply the victim of happenstance or that Lively merely chose him at random. Perhaps Oleen was too vocal or played too much of a leadership role among the strikers. Maybe he even suspected that Lively was an undercover operative for the agency. It does appear, however, that Lively went inside the establishment with plans to take another man's life, for that was the chosen method by which Lively was to be incarcerated, perhaps even including the specific man he shot.

---

42. Ancestry, www.ancestry.com.
43. Hardesty, "Better World," p. 216.
44. *Walsenburg World*, Walsenburg, Colorado, April 16, 1914.
45. Hardesty, "Better World," p. 216.

In a news report with the headline, "Striking Miner Shot Down," it stated, "Swanson Oleen, a striking miner, was shot fatally by Everett Lively, a mine owner's detective, in Pete Lage's saloon here."[46] This identical news story was wired around the state and appeared in numerous newspapers in cities throughout Colorado, such as Golden, Brandon, Yuma, Castle Rock, Dillon, and Hayden. "Mine owner's detective:" those three words were anathema to coal miners throughout the state of Colorado, in much the same way they had also been to miners in West Virginia. Charles E. Lively's secret service work no longer remained a secret. Once news of the shooting blanketed the state, Lively's cover was essentially blown. No longer could he move about freely, pose as a miner, and continue to gain intel as an undercover operative in the state of Colorado.

It was a perilous time to be living in Colorado. It was dangerous to be a mine guard, a striking miner, or a member of their families. It was also particularly risky to be a union organizer or a detective for Baldwin-Felts. With his detective status now known to many of those in the state's mining communities, Lively's life was in constant jeopardy every moment he remained in Colorado. However, residing under the protective custody of Huerfano County's Jeff Farr, Lively knew his life would be shielded from harm. In addition, while safely ensconced inside the stone walls of the jail in Walsenburg, the detective was also under the protective auspices of a county sheriff who hired over three hundred deputies, all of whom owed their allegiances and payroll to Jeff Farr's most powerful and wealthy ally, Colorado Fuel and Iron Company.

Perhaps Albert Felts also anticipated these results, because he obviously turned Lively's situation to the agency's distinct advantage. For the next sixteen months, Lively remained behind bars in the county jail, gathering intel for Baldwin-Felts from conversations he had with imprisoned miners, men who were thrown into jail by Jeff Farr for various reasons—or for little reason at all—during the period of his own confinement. No doubt many of the various miners, who were later arrested and shared a cell with Lively, talked freely of their local union activities in front of him, believing that his incarceration for murder likely severed all his friendly ties with Baldwin-Felts. It is also likely that Albert Felts was working closely with Sheriff Farr and other county officials, paying them handsomely to make sure Lively's case didn't readily come up for trial and that

---

46. *Eagle Valley Enterprise*, Eagle, Colorado, April 17, 1914.

Detective Lively could continue supplying them with information from the striking union miners. "Albert Felts the man for whom I was working," Lively said, "not wanting me to have a trial as he wanted an excuse for me to stay there in jail."[47] This unethical—and most likely, criminal—pact, concocted by Sheriff Jeff Farr, Albert Felts, and Charles E. Lively, certainly aided the corporate interests of Colorado Fuel and Iron Company.

Mere days after Swan Oleen succumbed to the wounds from Lively's gun, and while the agent was safely hidden away in a Huerfano County jail cell, hostilities came to a boiling point in nearby Ludlow. Near the mountains of southern Colorado, where thunderstorms often come and go at a moment's notice, another kind of storm was forming on the horizon. Less than twenty-four hours before the bloodshed occurred, many of the striking miners were enjoying the day, playing baseball games, and joyously celebrating the Greek New Year. "The following day the colonists were alarmed to see the militia setting up machine guns on Water Tank Hill, which was located to the south of the tent city and the buildings of the little town of Ludlow. The tension continued through the morning. Some of the women and children fled from the colony and took refuge in a large arroyo north of the tents."[48]

Nobody knows who took the first shot, but a bitter and deadly gun battle soon broke out between Linderfelt's National Guardsmen and armed strikers from the tent colony. This bloody fight continued throughout the day, taking the lives of no less than eight of the striking men and boys. "By afternoon, the miners were nearly out of ammunition and the militia was closing in fast," wrote the *Colorado Springs Gazette-Telegraph*. "But just as Linderfelt's men were about to overrun the colony, a train pulled up and blocked their advance. Linderfelt's men cursed and screamed at the train men, threatening to kill them. But the train men were union sympathizers, and they stopped long enough to allow hundreds of colonists to make a mad dash for the Black Hills."[49]

As nightfall approached, and the train no longer hindered their movements, the troops charged into the colony and set the tents ablaze "with kerosene-soaked brooms," the fire quickly

47. Hardesty, "Better World," p. 216.
48. Ree, "Walsenburg, Crossroads Town," pp. 75,76.
49. *Colorado Springs Gazette-Telegraph*, Colorado Springs, Colorado, April 24, 1994.

spreading from tent-to-tent.[50] Regarding the incident, William C. Blizzard wrote, "Darkness came and still the shooting continued. The women and children crawled out of their holes under cover of darkness and inched along on their bellies to the safety of a freight train. And then the militia swarmed in to Ludlow, set fire to the riddled tents and conducted a kind of war dance while they watched the flames eat into the April night."[51] Flames swept through the miners' canvas death-trap in what came to be forever known as the "Ludlow Massacre." Women and children, who'd earlier sought refuge from the bullets in their makeshift cellars, were suddenly unable to breathe from the smoke. After the conflagration left the tent colony in smoke and ruins, daylight revealed the grisly fact that two women and eleven children were dead, "the youngest a three-month-old baby," suffocated below ground, in this needless incident of labor violence. "One of the dead was Mrs. Pedelina Costa. Her two children died with her and that same night her husband had been killed by a National Guard bullet. The entire family was wiped out."[52]

University of Colorado Professor James H. Brewster, testifying before a federal commission on industrial relations said Lieutenant Karl Linderfelt was a "brute unfit to associate with anybody," and had he been removed, "Ludlow would never have happened."[53] The repercussions from this incident amounted to little more than a vast, public outcry, a public relations spectacle for John D. Rockefeller, and a federal hearing into industrial relations. That was all. Nobody was ever made to pay for these needless and tragic deaths. "Shortly before Ludlow, a grand jury had indicted the Colorado UMW leaders for alleged violation of the Sherman Anti-trust Act [Legislation passed in 1890, to eliminate business monopolies and to foster market competition], just as in West Virginia, and many miners were sent to jail during the struggle. But not one mine guard, company official or militiaman was ever punished in any way—yet again a parallel to the West Virginia situation."[54]

If must be stated, however, that Baldwin-Felts must also share a large portion of the blame for the Ludlow Massacre. They were certainly complicit. Even though the agency removed most of their agents from the region before the actual atrocities occurred, it was their machine guns which were employed by the militia to

50. Ibid.
51. Blizzard, "When Miners March," p. 104.
52. Ibid, p. 104.
53. *Fort Wayne Journal Gazette*, Fort Wayne, Indiana, December 8, 1914.
54. Blizzard, "When Miners March," p. 105.

devastate the strikers' tents. "Felts testified that he had been employed by the coal operators of the state for four years and that he had brot (sic) machine guns from West Virginia to be used in the Ludlow strike riots."[55] The weapons that Felts imported from their sieges in the southern West Virginia coalfields were still in the hands of Linderfelt's ruthless militia, men who used them with great effectiveness to inflict terror and bloodshed on the striking miners and their families at Ludlow. Moreover, Albert Felts wasn't the only Baldwin-Felts agent complicit in these brutal acts of labor violence. "C.B. Cunningham, a fellow agent, had manned the machine gun during an assault on striking miners camped at Ludlow...Six years later, when Felts and Cunningham climbed down from the train at Matewan Station, none of the local miners realized these two men had left Colorado with blood on their hands," wrote James Green in his book, *The Devil is Here in These Hills*.[56]

The atrocities which occurred at this Colorado strikers' encampment were so reprehensible, Lively even attempted to distance himself from the events of Ludlow, so much so that the detective falsely denied his time in the area when the tent colony was destroyed by fire. "I was not out there that soon. Let me see. I don't suppose I was," Lively testified. "They had some trouble at Ludlow before I went to Colorado, and I was not in that section. I was around La Veta and Walsenburg."[57] Even Charles E. Lively, who rarely agonized over any significant issues with conscience, had no desire to be in any way associated with this reckless slaughter.

Following the Ludlow Massacre, the incidents of violence only increased. Mines were attacked by miners, wielding rifles or dynamite. Buildings were set ablaze and mine guards were killed. The governor called out the entire Colorado National Guard and appealed to President Woodrow Wilson for the intervention of federal troops.

"A group of Baldwin-Felts men intercepted a car driven by a Federation of Labor official who was attempting to deliver high-powered rifles and 10,000 rounds of ammunition to the striking miners,"[58] John Velke wrote. It is quite likely that some of the information pertaining to this incident was gleaned and supplied to Baldwin-Felts by Charles E. Lively while he was still confined

55. *Leadville Herald Democrat*, Leadville, Colorado, May 20, 1920.
56. Green, "The Devil is Here in These Hills," p. 207.
57. Hardesty, "Better World," p. 223.
58. Velke, "The True Story of the Baldwin-Felts Detective Agency," p. 187.

*Memorial in Ludlow, Colorado, to honor the victims of the
Ludlow Massacre.*

(Author's collection)

behind bars. At the end of those sixteen months, when Lively was finally brought before a judge, he was given "ten days" for "involuntary manslaughter," credited for time served, and ordered to leave the state of Colorado, something Lively needed to do anyway in order to ensure his own safety.[59]

From there, Lively's work for Baldwin-Felts took him to Missouri around 1915, where he stayed for "possibly a year. I was in the state of Missouri," he said, "a good part of the time."[60] Next, his agency's assignments took him to Oklahoma, Kansas, and Illinois. From his World War I draft registration it is known that Lively was living in Kansas in June 1917. Given that Charles E. Lively seldom, if ever, appeared ashamed of his duties while working for Baldwin-Felts, his response regarding the specific location of his work in Illinois is indeed puzzling. For some reason known only to Lively, when questioned about Illinois, he deliberately sought to avoid sharing anything in the way of details. "Unless that is absolutely necessary, I hate awful to divulge that place," Lively testified. "I can state what State it was. I don't hesitate to say that it was in the state of Illinois."[61] In the future murder trial in Williamson, West Virginia, when asked about his undercover work in Illinois, Lively repeated this bizarre behavior in regards to the Land of Lincoln. Lively testified that he would "rather not specify" his activities in that state.[62]

Much of his time after leaving Colorado, along with the dates and details of the specific duties Lively performed in these states, is still a mystery. But there can be no question that his undercover work for Baldwin-Felts also involved some matters of labor unrest. Killing, obviously, was an easy chore for Lively. Moreover, the detective always found ways to justify the incidents when he took a life. Therefore, the refusal to talk about his spy work in Illinois is indeed strange behavior, even for a complex, but a proudly unapologetic individual. It is probable, however, that whatever undercover duties, or crimes, Lively performed in Illinois may not have been protected under a statute of limitations, or those activities might have been such that Lively feared he could still face some grudgingly personal retribution for his actions or misdeeds.

59. Testimony at the Matewan defendants' murder trial in Williamson, West Virginia, 1921.
60. Ibid.
61. Ibid.
62. *East Liverpool Evening Review*, East Liverpool, Ohio, February 26, 1921.

Ultimately, those details were forever lost at the hands of Estil L. Meadows, Baldwin's chief clerk, who later inherited the agency. Since "Pinkerton's National Detective Agency and the William J. Burns International Detective Agency had already been subpoenaed and were expected to face tough questioning regarding their use of secret service men," it is believed that William G. Baldwin ordered Meadows to destroy the agency's records not long before the founder died.[63] In so doing, they sought to avoid a situation in which Baldwin-Felts would be subjected to the same type of intrusive Congressional scrutiny and subpoenas into their own labor espionage practices that the other detective agencies faced. It may also be presumed Meadows' willful destruction of records was a deliberate effort to conceal and protect the names and reputations of those who employed the services of Baldwin-Felts. Despite those missing or destroyed records, it is known that Charles E. Lively left that region of the country and headed eastward, returning to West Virginia around 1920.

63. Velke, John, "The True Story of the Baldwin-Felts Detective Agency.

CHAPTER 5

Returning to West Virginia

After Charles E. Lively completed his work for Baldwin-Felts in Colorado, was released from his extended jail incarceration, and fled the state for his own safety, his largely unknown undercover work took him to several other western states. Many of these places were detailed in his 1921 Senate testimony.

Despite his travels for Baldwin Felts from about 1912 to 1920, Lively maintained a residence for his wife and family in Bluefield, West Virginia, a place he would revisit occasionally, taking brief furloughs from his undercover work. Lively even returned to Bluefield in April 1918, taking time to briefly visit his severely ill father at Davis Creek, who succumbed to his condition in February 1919. Upon finishing his mysterious duties in those western states, labor hostilities once again flared up in West Virginia in 1920. As one of their most trusted and effective agents, it was believed that Lively could also be of great benefit at home. "I think I first went to Mingo County in January or February," Lively said.[1]

Once more, Lively posed as a union coal miner when he was assigned to investigate the robbery of a company store in Red Jacket and the burning of a coal tipple and coal washer in Chattaroy. In the course of his investigation, Lively attempted to win the friendship and trust of those alleged to have committed the crimes. Upon learning details regarding these incidents, Lively would send the information he acquired to his superiors at Baldwin-Felts. However, West Virginia coal mining communities were small; gossip was rampant and secrecy was rare.

Along with that, the managers of the company stores often worked directly for the mine owners, and one of their primary duties was to keep tabs on the local residents, to know their business and to be aware if any union organizing efforts were underway. In addition, the coal companies generally had no

1. *Bluefield (WV) City Directory 1919-1920. Charleston Daily Mail*, Charleston, West Virginia, April 3, 1918. Hardesty, "Better World," p. 143.

knowledge of the detectives' true identities; therefore, it was difficult for an agent to pass along the intelligence details he learned without his actions somehow being exposed as a Baldwin-Felts operative. There was also the risk of being discovered by union sympathizers, miners or their family members, ones who also spent time at the store, or those who were often secretly supportive of their cause but still unknown by the coal companies.

"They had a box number that no one knew about, only theirselves," Lively testified. "Sometimes I sent my reports to Williamson, and when I did, I would make it out in a girl's name and address it to a box number, and the man stationed in Williamson would look after that." As a "secret service" operative for Baldwin-Felts, it was commonplace for a detective to be completely on his own while out on an assignment. Most of the detectives who worked undercover had no knowledge whatsoever of their fellow agents. Lively stated, "We have positive instructions not to reveal our identity to anyone." He later said, "None of those secret-service men working for the Baldwin-Felts Detective Agency knows any of the others."[2]

Since the agency required secrecy from its operatives and the coal companies had no knowledge of their identities, it was not unusual for the owners to occasionally terminate one of the detectives for seemingly becoming too sociable with the pro-union miners. This required the agents to hide their anti-union views when they were around those loyal to the coal operators, the ones most opposed to the unions, despite the fact they essentially shared the same beliefs. As evidence of this fact, while working the case in Chattaroy, Lively was employed by Howard Collories Company, but approximately a month later, the detective was abruptly fired by the company superintendent. "I was boarding at the same place with this man that was suspected of burning the tipple and was associating with him," Lively explained, "and him not knowing who I was, not knowing I was doing secret-service work, I suppose he just thought I was too friendly with him."[3]

After being fired, his work for Baldwin-Felts soon took him to Williamson, Merrimac, and eventually to Matewan. The termination for getting too close to union activists also worked in Lively's favor, making those in the UMWA think the detective was loyal to the cause and numbered as one of their own.

2. Ibid, p. 145, 155.
3. Ibid, p. 145.

Overwhelmingly convinced of Lively's loyalty, union officials, such as Charley Workman, even started coming to him for assistance in the organizing of locals and obtaining members at War Eagle, Glen Alum, and Mohawk.[4]

At the time, Lively was a member of the Stone Mountain local and earned "$225 and expenses" per month from Baldwin-Felts.[5] The evidence would suggest that he was also firmly establishing himself as one of District 17's most trusted members, since it was obvious he needed no specific invitation to visit the UMW's headquarters in Charleston, West Virginia. "Lively had immediately joined the union and became one of its most active members, organizing meetings, swearing in new recruits, planning strategies. He had participated enthusiastically in the strike convention, posing with Mother Jones and the convention leaders for a photograph."[6] Lively's infiltration of the union had been so convincing and successful, it appears that many of those in the rank and file, along with a number of high-placed union officials from the region, envisioned the undercover detective as a future leader within the district hierarchy.

The UMWA leadership was firmly committed to the establishment of the union throughout every community that dug coal from the ground in West Virginia. However, the coal companies across the state were just as equally committed to stopping those union organizing efforts. "A representative of the Associated Press was en route from Bluefield to Kenova via the Norfolk & Western Railroad. During that trip he engaged a prominent coal operator (then operating in that field) in conversation. "'We are not going to fight the union like we have been fighting it,' the operator confided. 'We have been spending fabulous sums to hire guards to keep the organizers out, but we are not going to do that any longer. We are going to secure indictments against the officers and active members of the union, throw them into jail, deny bail, prosecute them, and even if we do not secure many convictions, we will keep the union bled of funds and break them that way.'"[7] This was strategy the West Virginia coal operators vigorously pursued for most of the decade, although these executives never fully abandoned their tried, trusted, and often brutal, mine guard system of espionage and intimidation.

---

4. Ibid, p. 147.
5. Ibid, p. 148.
6. Lon Savage "Thunder in the Mountains: The West Virginia Mine War, 1920-21," (The University of Pittsburgh Press, 1990), p. 33.
7. Mooney, "Struggle in the Coal Fields," p. 86.

City of Matewan, West Virginia, taken around the time of the shootout.

(West Virginia State Archives)

All the while, Lively continued to make a name for himself in Matewan, attending meetings and making speeches. "He was loud in his denunciation of the gunman system and advised the miners to join the union and fight for their rights."[8] He also urged the miners to "cut out the blood and thunder stuff—the killing" and to use more discretion in their efforts to successfully unionize.[9] When tensions continued to build and the battle lines became more clearly drawn between the coal operators and the miners, Workman and others began pushing Lively to get more involved in union organizing efforts.

"I didn't want to do that," Lively explained. "I didn't like the idea any more than just to keep my identity uncovered; but if I bought a restaurant or some kind of a business there, or got some kind of a job there, then that gave me an excuse for staying there, so I could have a plausible excuse for not going out and doing any work for them."[10] So, it was decided. Lively acquired

8. Ibid, p. 72.
9. *East Liverpool Daily Review*, East Liverpool, Ohio, February 26, 1921.
10. Hardesty, "Better World," p. 152, 153.

the lower floor of a building on the east end of Matewan to use for his restaurant, a place that was already furnished with all the costly restaurant equipment. In order to make it run, the detective simply needed to purchase the food and supplies for his business. In another brilliant moment of strategic planning from the clever Baldwin-Felts detective, he rented the building from the United Mine Workers, which used the space above his restaurant for their offices.

According to Lively's own sworn Senate testimony, he didn't acquire the business until after the seven detectives were shot down in Matewan. However, the accounts of Howard Lee and Fred Mooney appear to contradict Lively's claims about when he first became the restaurant's proprietor. In his book, Howard Lee said, "Lively had gone to Matewan and opened a restaurant three weeks before the Massacre, and remained there until the first trial."[11]

On May 6, 1920, Fred Mooney and Bill Blizzard spoke to a great crowd of striking miners who assembled for a rally in Matewan during a huge rain storm. After the meeting was over and they all met in Lively's restaurant, the agent did his best to persuade Mooney, his old childhood friend, to go to his home and spend the night there. "However, somewhere in my subconscious mind," Mooney wrote, "there lurked a suspicion that all was not right with Lively. Acting upon this 'hunch,' I did not go to his home."[12] From the record, it is obvious that Mooney had every reason to be skeptical of his boyhood friend. Poverty was rampant among the coal miners of Mingo County. Yet, there was Lively, who strangely disappeared from the area for many years, a person raised in starkly-similar circumstances to Mooney, with money enough to purchase a restaurant. It is therefore surprising that a great many others didn't recognize that 'all was not right' with Charles E. Lively. This is clearly more tangible evidence of Lively's remarkable skills at deceit and persuasion.

In the days that followed, Lively's restaurant continued to be a popular gathering place for the strikers. Thinking they were in a friendly and like-minded environment, the miners, no doubt, talked freely of their plans while eating their meals. It is also certain that UMWA officials, coming downstairs from their headquarters, often failed to discreetly halt their union-related

11. Lee, "Bloodletting in Appalachia," p. 62.
12. Mooney, "Struggle in the Coal Fields," p. 72.

Charles E. Lively on the right. His brother, Arthur Lively, on the left. The night before the Matewan shootout, Lively spent the night at Arthur's house in Shrewsbury, West Virginia, before traveling to the USWA headquarters in Charleston the following morning, where he learned of the bloody shootout. It is believed Charles is approximately in his 40s to early 50s in this picture.

(Courtesy of Larry Lively)

conversations when entering Lively's establishment. After all, everybody believed the cordial hash-slinger was one of them.

Using the restaurant as a prop for his ongoing drama of labor espionage, the detective acquired more and more intel about the union's organizing activities. He also participated in the planning of their activities, sometimes packing the meals the striking miners would carry while engaged in these missions. Lively even supplied them with cayenne pepper, something they used to hide their scent from the detectives' bloodhounds.[13] At the same time, Lively profited financially from his deceit, deriving both a substantial income from his undercover work and also earning money as a restaurant entrepreneur. He also shared much of the critical information he gathered with his superiors at Baldwin-Felts.

On May 18, 1920, Lively traveled to Shrewsbury, West Virginia, and spent the afternoon at the house of his brother, Arthur. After sharing his sibling's hospitality for the night, Lively awoke and resumed his journey to Charleston, continuing his mission of acquiring more intel at the headquarters of the United Mine Workers. On that day, however, everything changed for the UMWA, throughout both the state of West Virginia and across the rest of the country. Baldwin-Felts' most effective undercover agent was about to receive the most important assignment of his career. That one assignment altered Charles E. Lively's life forever.

---

13. *Bluefield Daily Telegraph*, Bluefield, West Virginia, August 6, 1921.

CHAPTER 6

Bloodletting in Matewan

In 1920, union organizing activities had reached such a fevered pitch in southern West Virginia, coal operators knew they needed to organize some kind of muscled push-back against the strikers. On May 19, 1920, the Norfolk & Western locomotive, Number 29, thundered up to the depot in Matewan, West Virginia. The passenger train carried several heavily armed men from Baldwin-Felts, including Albert and Lee Felts, brothers of Thomas L. Felts, co-owner of the agency. Operating under orders from Stone Mountain Coal Company, these agents planned to evict about a half-dozen striking miners from their company-owned homes at gunpoint.

Earlier, Albert Felts had offered Mayor Cabell Testerman one-thousand dollars to place machine guns in Matewan, on rooftops on Mate Street, purely in his interest to "preserve the peace."[1] The mayor rejected the bribe and admonished the agent to make sure his men strictly obeyed the local ordinances while conducting their unseemly business in his town. On this day, Albert Felts carried a letter from his brother, Thomas L. Felts. Knowing Sid Hatfield, the Matewan Chief of Police, might prove to be a substantial roadblock to their plans, Tom Felts proposed making a financial appeal, a bribe if you will, to urge Sid to join their side.

"If you make a deal with him I think you should suggest some means of bringing about a controversy or misunderstanding of some sort which will result in a split between him and the bunch which would look plausible and give him an opportunity of turning against them and telling them where to head in," Felts explained. "Because that is what we will expect if we make a deal."[2]

Upon their arrival, the men of Baldwin-Felts made their way to the friendly confines of the Urias Hotel and were greeted by Anse Hatfield—not to be mistaken for Devil Anse Hatfield,

1. Shogan, "The Battle of Blair Mountain," p. 20.
2. Ibid, p. 22.

famed for his less-than-friendly feudal activities with the equally unfriendly McCoy clan. Anse was, however, related to the famed leader of the Hatfield-McCoy feud and was also a cousin to the town's smiling Chief of Police. Supportive of the agents' cause, Anse Hatfield served lunch to the Baldwin-Felts men and the agents dined peaceably, waiting on the arrival of other detectives who were due to come into town on the next train.

Not long after lunch, Albert Felts, now accompanied by a dozen other agents, decided it was time for the detectives to start the process of evictions. The agents were Albert and Lee Felts, Bill Salter, C.B. Cunningham, R.C. Buchanon, Oscar Bennett, J.W. Ferguson, C.T. Higgins, A.J. Boorher, E.O. Powell, John McDowell, and brothers, J.R. Anderson and G.A. Anderson. "Nearly all 'have been tried and can be relied on,' Tom Felts had written to his brother, Albert."[3] Three automobiles, loaded down with a baker's dozen of men and guns, drove to the striking miners' Stone Mountain Coal Company homes, located just outside of town. Once there, the agents began dragging the miners' belongings and furniture outside. They tossed those items into piles in the middle of the street while some of the other agents stood watch with pistols and rifles to keep the helpless and angry miners, along with their distraught wives and children at bay. The guns also were to protect themselves from any outside interference or attacks.

Removing people from their company-owned homes was busy and dangerous work, and the agents went about their task heartily, no doubt spurred on by the curses and cries coming from the lips of the miners and their families. "The Baldwin-Felts men intended to finish in time to make the 5:15 train back to Bluefield."[4]

Not long after the agents started evicting the miners, they were confronted by Matewan Mayor Cabell Testerman and his city's Chief of Police, Sid Hatfield. After inspecting their papers, Testerman and Hatfield claimed the eviction warrants were bogus. Albert Felts challenged the two men's jurisdictional rights to enforce the law outside the Matewan city limits. Their verbal dispute lasted for several minutes before the agents returned to their work and the Mayor and Hatfield went back to town.

Once back in Matewan, the outraged mayor and Sid got on the phone to Williamson and soon learned the agents' eviction

3. Shogan, "The Battle of Blair Mountain," p. 1.
4. Ibid, p. 21.

warrants were indeed suspect. A man from Sheriff Blankenship's office notified Testerman that warrants were being issued to arrest the detectives. Those warrants were due to arrive on "the same train the Baldwin-Felts men planned to take back to Bluefield."[5]

Mayor Testerman, expecting there might be trouble, asked Hugh Combs, a lay preacher of the gospel, to pick several "sober-minded men." Men to be deputized as special officers to back up Hatfield should any violence ensue.[6] Mr. Combs, "the self-proclaimed minister later commented he planned to kill a few detectives himself."[7] Of course, that was fine with the Chief of Police, who didn't care as much about the men's sober-mindedness as he did their ability to work the lever on a Winchester. "The police chief and his boyish-looking deputy, Ed Chambers, deputized a dozen men Hugh Combs had rounded up and told them to gather in the hardware store owned by Ed's father, 'Daddy' Reece Chambers."[8] No doubt there were other miners in Matewan who also learned of the impending trouble and brought their guns to town, manning various locations nearby.

Hatfield's earlier call for arrest warrants was overheard by a couple of phone operators, Elsie Chambers and Mae Chafin, and no doubt carried to the friends of the agents the moment Sid declared he would "kill those sons of bitches before they get out of Matewan."[9] However, the threats and bold talk on that bleak and damp afternoon were not only limited to the friends and loyalists of Sid Hatfield. Albert C. Felts and his allies also were guilty of their own brand of menacing invectives. "William Bowman stated that he had a talk with Lee Toler," Lively wrote, "who was then working for Jeff Hatfield, and says that he had a talk with A.C. on that day and that A.C. told him (Toler) that he was going to kill Sid Hatfield and Ezra Fry before No. 16 ran that evening."[10]

Around 4 PM, the townspeople, armed with Winchesters or other long guns, lurked in various locations around town, waiting for the agents' return. The battle lines were drawn and the tinder was set in place. All that was needed to create an

5. Ibid, p. 23.
6. Ibid, p. 23.
7. Savage, "Thunder in the Mountains," p. 21.
8. Green, "The Devil is Here in These Hills," p. 207.
9. Shogan, "The Battle of Blair Mountain," p. 95.
10. #9 Communication, Thomas Felts' Papers, Eastern Regional Coal Archives, Bluefield, West Virginia.

Appalachian inferno was a tiny spark. Unlike a traditional Western novel, there were no heroes in this story, or in the events that later sprang from what transpired at the Matewan Massacre on that bloody afternoon.

Upon finishing their unsavory business of evictions, the agents' cars returned to the Urias Hotel. The detectives cased their rifles and sat down to dinner, waiting for Norfolk & Western's train Number 16 to take them home. Unknown to them, some of the men were eating their last meal. "Only four guards, the Felts brothers, Bill Salter, and C.B. Cunningham were licensed to carry pistols. The others carried high-power rifles, for which no license was then required."[11]

Despite some cross words from the miners, the Mayor, and the Chief of Police, their day had gone largely without incident. After enjoying a leisurely dinner and pleased with their day's efforts, the detectives, some carrying their rifle cases, left the hotel and began walking toward the depot. Clouds darkened the afternoon sky and a light rain began to fall upon the town. Some of the detectives were dressed in yellow raincoats. Before they arrived, Sid Hatfield intercepted the detectives on the street and informed Albert Felts that he and his party were under arrest and that the warrants would soon be delivered on the coming train.

"Felts laughed. 'Sid,' he said, 'I've got a warrant for you too. I'm going to take you with me to Bluefield.'" This pair of dangerous men and cordial enemies eyed each other like two bulls in a corral full of heifers, yet each individual was still somewhat amused by the other. "Hatfield laughed, too, and both men, smiling as if they were playing out a practical joke, walked down the street together, the other detectives trailing behind."[12]

Felts and Hatfield stopped just outside the door of Chambers Hardware. Mayor Testerman joined them there as well, the mayor contesting the authenticity of the warrant Felts presented for Hatfield's arrest. Inside the hardware store, several armed miners were waiting, including Isaac Brewer, who was then a friend of Sid's. "I was surrounded by detectives," Hatfield later testified. "Behind me stood Isaac Brewer; beside me Mayor Testerman."[13]

---

11. Lee, "Bloodletting in Appalachia," p. 53.
12. Shogan, "The Battle of Blair Mountain," p. 21.
13. Testimony at the murder trial for those who killed Albert C. Felts in Williamson, West Virginia, in 1921.

What happened next will forever be the subject of conjecture and dispute. Despite the bitter and inflammatory allegations which arose from each side of the conflict, nobody has ever conclusively determined which party fired the first shot or from where that initial shot originated. However, there has never been any dispute whatsoever to the fact that Albert Felts and Mayor Testerman were clearly the first victims to go down from the earliest pistol blasts. It is also apparent that Albert Felts still believed the four licensed, pistol-carrying agents gave him the upper hand if any kind of armed dispute arose, revealing that A.C. Felts truly had no idea of the substantial number of armed men stationed around the town. At this time, the agents of Baldwin-Felts experienced something unusual: They were seriously outgunned.

Sid Hatfield later claimed that Albert Felts shot the mayor with a gun from inside the pocket of his coat. Other witnesses testified that Hatfield shot the mayor, simply to get the man's wife, a claim that is truly doubtful since it is unlikely any man would risk entering into a potentially deadly gun battle, in which he himself might die, simply to satisfy his carnal desires. The evidence suggests, however; that the first shot from Sid Hatfield's gun mortally wounded Albert Felts by striking him in the head. Albert, field manager for the agency, once bragged to a sheriff's deputy, "I am going to break this union on Tug River if it sends 100 men to hell and costs a million dollars."[14] At the time he made the statement, Albert had no way of knowing that his life proved to be the first one taken and that, by the end of the day, he was a tenth of the way to meeting his stated goal.

When Felts and Testerman were felled from single gunshots, it immediately triggered shooting from all quarters. Rifle and pistol fire erupted from numerous locations in Matewan: upper story windows, alleys, and rooftops. The few, armed Baldwin-Felts agents desperately returned fire and the others fled, scrambling for their lives. The street filled with smoke from the weapons and the bloodbath in Matewan began.

In the next twenty minutes of carnage, over one-hundred shots were taken. Seven agents were killed and others wounded. Two civilians also met their deaths from gunfire and several were wounded. The mortally wounded Mayor was taken to the hospital in Welch and lingered until evening before succumbing to his wounds.

14. Shogan, "The Battle of Blair Mountain," p. 106.

"Why did they shoot me?" were Cabell Testerman's last words. "I can't see why they shot me."[15]

"Testerman told Albert Felts the warrant on which the detectives were trying to take me out of the county was fictitious," Hatfield later explained. "At this Felts whipped out his gun and shot Testerman, then swung his gun half over his shoulder and shot Brewer. I pulled my two guns; one was knocked out of my hand by a bullet. At the same time another bullet tore through my hat, flipping it off. I started firing just as quickly as I could."[16]

Isaac Brewer was wounded, hit in the right chest.[17] It is believed the shot came from either the gun of Albert Felts or C.B. Cunningham. "Still on his feet, Brewer pulled his own gun, only to have it shot from his hand. Gravely wounded he retreated to the back of the hardware store to stop the blood."[18]

"Isaac Brewer told me he was hit in the first volley," Lively wrote in one of his secretive memos, "and that he thinks Cunningham shot him."[19]

Upon seeing his older brother fall, Lee Felts drew his gun and traded multiple gunshots with Art Williams, with neither of the men hitting their target. However, a slug from Reece Chambers' rifle was right on target and hit Lee Felts in the neck. Lee hit the ground dead. It is also believed that, before he died, one of the shots from Lee's gun killed Tot Tinsley, a young, unarmed miner.[20]

After Reece Chambers killed Lee Felts, Art Williams snatched away one of Felts' pistols and saw that it was empty. Kicking another one free from Felts' clenched hand, he saw it still contained cartridges and ran over to a mortally wounded A.J. Boorher and shot the man at point-blank range, the crimson blowback spattering all over the weapon. Boorher is also credited with the killing of Bob Mullins, although it is not certain what gun Boorher might have used, since he was one of the agents purportedly not carrying a handgun.[21]

15. Ibid, p. 25.
16. Testimony at the murder trial for those who killed Albert C. Felts in Williamson, West Virginia, in 1921.
17. Savage, "Thunder in the Mountains," p. 24.
18. Ibid, p. 24.
19. Thomas Felts' Papers, Eastern Regional Coal Archives, Bluefield, West Virginia.
20. Savage, "Thunder in the Mountains," pp. 22, 23.
21. Testimony at the murder trial for those who killed Albert C. Felts in Williamson, West Virginia, in 1921. Savage, "Thunder in the Mountains," p. 23. Velke, "The True Story of the Baldwin-Felts Detective Agency," p. 220.

Detective E.O. Powell was killed early in the conflict, with it still uncertain who was primarily responsible for his death.[22] "[Agent] Higgins is said to have started into the rear of a doctor's office to get away, but someone standing inside the office knocked him in the head with a gallon jug and he fell backward into the street, where he was shot in the first hail of bullets."[23]

In a conflicting report, Lively later testified that Henry Haywood was the man who struck Higgins in the head with a chloroform bottle, but Lively maintained that it was Art Williams who fired Felts' gun into the head of Detective Higgins, not A.J. Boorher.[24]

Detective Bill Salter fired back at his attackers until his pistol went empty. Once he was out of bullets, the fearful detective ran and hid in a garbage can until nightfall. Later that night, sensing it was finally safe to emerge from his hiding spot, Salter hobbled out of the can due to his loss of circulation. From there, he slipped into the darkness, swam the Tug River, and escaped, only later to reappear as a major player in the continuing acts of West Virginia coal violence.

"The two Andersons and Buchanon ran through a store and down the railroad tracks toward Williamson and escaped."[25] G.A. Anderson was later hospitalized and treated for a bullet wound. In telling of his escape, Anderson [G.A.] said, "My brother and I jumped a fence and ran into a vacant house which we found occupied by men with rifles and revolvers. I received my shoulder wounds there, but we managed to escape to the next house, where no one was home. As the train pulled in, we managed to escape in time to board the last car and were not again discovered."[26]

It is not documented what wounds R.C. Buchanon may have received, but the detective had only returned from the war in Europe about a year earlier. He was "a highly decorated World War I veteran," who was responsible for "singlehandedly capturing three Germans while under grenade, automatic rifle, and machine-gun fire. As he recuperated in the hospital, he told

---

22. Savage, "Thunder in the Mountains," p. 23.
23. *The Kingsport Times*, Kingsport, Tennessee, July 6, 1920.
24. #9 Communication. Thomas Felts' Papers, Eastern Regional Coal Archives, Bluefield, West Virginia.; Testimony at the murder trial for those who killed Albert C. Felts in Williamson, West Virginia, in 1921.
25. Lee, "Bloodletting in Appalachia," p. 53.
26. *Bluefield Daily Telegraph*, Bluefield, West Virginia, May 21, 1920

visitors that the ambush and massacre at Matewan was unequalled by any of his experiences at the European front."[27]

J.W. Ferguson was hit in the first volley of gunfire, seriously wounded, and sought refuge at the nearby home of Mary Duty. "He collapsed in a wicker chair and pleaded with Mrs. Duty to go for a doctor. When she returned, she discovered him lying dead in the alley behind her house. There were fresh bullet holes in his body that coincided with the bullet holes found in the back of her wicker chair."[28]

According to later testimony by Lively, Ferguson was shot by Fred Burgraff. "Ferguson did not show any nerve at all but begged for his life, and said, 'please don't kill me, I am unarmed, and if you don't kill me I will never do any more work of this kind'. Mooney said that Burgrass (sic) said, 'You have went too far now, you have got to go to h---' and shot him." In addition, Lively wrote that he "heard Bob McCoy say he was with the bunch that killed Ferguson and that Fred Burgrass (sic) and Elihu Young both shot him with rifles, after he had plead (sic) for his life."[29]

John McDowell, another Baldwin-Felts man who supposedly wasn't armed, testified that he fired "two or three shots himself," before fleeing the scene.[30] His life was spared because he dared to ask a woman for the fastest way out of town. "Pointing to the river, she said, 'Split the creek.'"[31] Upon receiving her answer, McDowell sprinted to the water's edge, dived into the flow, and swam to the safety of Kentucky while his colleagues were shot down and died in the bloody streets on the West Virginia side of the Tug River.

"Cunningham was the last guard to fall. Although mortally wounded by the first volley, he propped his fast-failing body against a lightpole and emptied his pistol at his attackers. With his pistol empty, his knees buckled, and he slumped to the sidewalk."[32]

In Detective Cunningham's brief, remaining moments before passing into eternity, he boldly watched Sid Hatfield approach

27. Velke, "The True Story of the Baldwin-Felts Detective Agency," p. 221.
28. Ibid, p. 221.
29. Testimony at the murder trial for those who killed Albert C. Felts in Williamson, West Virginia, in 1921.; #9 Communication. Thomas Felts' Papers, Eastern Regional Coal Archives, Bluefield, West Virginia.
30. For a full discussion about John McDowell, see Appendix A.; *Galveston Tribune*, Galveston, Texas, February 12, 1921.
31. Shogan, "The Battle of Blair Mountain," p. 25.
32. Lee, "Bloodletting in Appalachia," p. 55.

him and lift the gun to trigger a final, deadly slug into his skull. After killing the man and speaking to those gathered around him, Sid remarked that the "son-of-a-bitch sure had a heap of guts."[33] "So many miners fired at C.B. Cunningham that no one could claim clear credit for this death. His body was riddled with bullets, his head half blown off."[34] The agent's death in Matewan finally reunited him with those departed souls in the afterlife, whose lives Cunningham may have taken while manning the machine guns in Ludlow, Colorado.

Oscar Bennett's life was reportedly saved because he left the other agents and went to purchase a pack of cigarettes. Since Bennett arrived in town on the later train and failed to eat lunch with the other detectives, those in Matewan failed to easily recognize him. Upon hearing the gunshots, he ducked into the depot and mingled among those passengers waiting to catch the train. Bennett escaped death on the Norfolk & Western.

The bodies of the fallen detectives remained in the streets until later that evening. Many of the dead were riddled with additional bullets. The townspeople rummaged through their pockets, snatching away wallets, cash, rings, watches, and other valuables from their corpses. It is also alleged that Sid Hatfield later took sole possession of the guns pried from the cold, dead hands of Albert and Lee Felts.[35]

Witnesses aboard the 5:15 train claimed that they saw several incidences of drinking and celebrations taking place over the bodies of the slain agents. It is said that Detective Ferguson's body was carried on a makeshift litter, "fashioned out of Winchesters. As they passed through town one of the miners nodded at the rifles and said: 'They brought them in here and they're going out on them.'"[36] When the next train arrived and Sid Hatfield received the arrest warrants, which just arrived there from Williamson, the Matewan Chief of Police walked over to the dead body of Albert Felts and said, "Now, you son of a bitch, I'll serve it on you."[37]

In the aftermath of the day's shooting, there were other acts of nearby violence. "Following the fatal fighting at Matewan another shooting was reported from Lynn, a neighboring mining village. 'Bud' McCoy and his brother, said to be Baldwin-Felts

33. Velke, "The True Story of the Baldwin-Felts Detective Agency," p. 220.
34. Shogan, "The Battle of Blair Mountain," p. 26.
35. Lee, "Bloodletting in Appalachia," p. 56.
36. Shogan, "The Battle of Blair Mountain," p. 25.
37. Savage, "Thunder in the Mountains," p. 24.

detectives were fired on from the mountainside. 'Bud' was wounded in the thigh."[38] Anger, fear, and confusion reigned as night fell upon Bloody Mingo. Searchers were even dragging the river, searching for the body of John McDowell, or others who were believed to be drowned.

The locals were also fearful of reports that Thomas Felts was headed to Matewan, accompanied by a large contingent of armed detectives. "Sid Hatfield expected a counterattack and asked for help from Sheriff Blankenship, who deputized a formidable force of a hundred men to defend Matewan. As the train carrying Felts and his agents barreled down the Tug River Valley, it seemed certain that an even bloodier battle would soon erupt. The locomotive engineer had learned, however, that a gun party waited to greet Felts and his men, and he rushed his train past Matewan Station without stopping, despite furious protests from the agents, and rolled on toward Williamson."[39]

Also fearing the possibility of more violence, the governor ordered the state police to Matewan to restore order. However, their presence did nothing to deter the dozens of armed miners, who were seen patrolling the hillsides, carefully watching the arrival of anyone on the incoming trains.[40] In a statement from Thomas Felts, who lost two of his brothers in the conflict, the vice president of the agency stated, "Not being satisfied with murder, the helpless bodies of their victims were shot, maltreated, and robbed as they lay on the ground. In their greed for plunder, they even stole the Masonic Shriners' pin from the lapel of my brother's coat."[41]

"The bodies of the detectives lay on the street until Blankenship and W.O. Porter, the mayor of Williamson, arrived on the 7:15 P.M. train and saw to it that the corpses were put on a train back to Williamson."[42] The remains of the slain Baldwin-Felts detectives were delivered to their various families by train. The remains of Albert and Lee Felts were claimed by Thomas Felts and buried near his family home in Galax, Virginia. Today, there are no existing West Virginia death certificates to be found for the seven fallen agents, because the dead were transported to the Ball Funeral Home in Williamson, West Virginia, which suffered a devastating flood later that same year, depriving the world of additional clarity and truth regarding the conflict.

38. *Logansport Pharos Tribune*, Logansport, Indiana, May 21, 1920.
39. Green, "The Devil is Here in These Hills," p. 212.
40. *Bluefield Daily Telegraph*, Bluefield, West Virginia, May 21, 1920.
41. *Roanoke World News*, Roanoke, Virginia, May 29, 1920.
42. Shogan, "The Battle of Blair Mountain," p. 26.

The side of the building that was the U.S. Post Office during the Matewan shootout. A number of these buildings still have the bullet holes from May 19, 1920.

(Author's collection)

Although Charles E. Lively wasn't in Matewan, West Virginia, the day of the actual shooting, it does appear that, like the Ludlow Massacre in Colorado, tragedy routinely followed in the undercover detective's wake. Perhaps it should also be considered no coincidence that death and violence routinely seemed to raise their ugly heads anywhere close to where Lively chose to take up an extended residence.

After spending the night with his brother, Lively was in Charleston at the UMWA headquarters when he first learned about the killings in Matewan. It can also be presumed that, along with working another case, Lively was given advance warning of the agency's plans to carry out those evictions in Matewan, and his sudden trip to Charleston might have simply been a means to avoid the uncomfortable position of taking sides in the actions of Albert Felts and the other detectives. Lively first learned the news of the violence in Matewan in the form of a telegram from Charley Workman. Lively later claimed that he was there at the union headquarters with Fred Mooney, although Mooney's U.S. Senate committee testimony said that Fred only learned about the events in Matewan from a telephone call to his residence. In addition, when questioned about the telegram, Lively said, "I sent Mooney after it. Down to the Western Union office."[43]

It does, however, seem unlikely that any individual, involved in any way, in the labor unrest in West Virginia during that period would fail to remember where he was located when he first learned about the violence in Matewan. Perhaps it will never be possible to fully explain these two conflicting accounts. It is, however, possible that both accounts were true and perhaps, as a leader of USWA's District 17, Mooney already received the alarming telephone call before he went to the headquarters that evening. Perhaps Mooney didn't choose to share the information regarding the shootout with the others and then was later presented with the telegram.

When asked about how the information from the telegram was received, Lively replied, "Well, most of them agreed that it was a mighty good thing, seemed to enjoy it; Charles Batley especially." Lively further stated that Batley was "dancing around the floor and said it was the best news he had had for a long while."[44] Although he might have found the news from Matewan

43. Hardesty, "Better World," p. 149.
44. Ibid, p. 149.

tragic and distasteful, Lively's precarious status as an undercover operative didn't allow him any room to reveal his true feelings about the incident and the loss of his friend, Albert Felts. "Lively was obliged to sit and pretend that he, too, was happy over that carnage."[45]

45. Blizzard, William C., "Coal's Dramatic Period," *Charleston Gazette-Mail*, Charleston, West Virginia, June 16, 1963.

CHAPTER 7

Agent No. 9

In the days and weeks immediately following the Matewan Massacre, Lively's restaurant on the town's east end became a crucial meeting place for both parties in this bloody and bitter war. Lively was working both sides of the street, not only acquiring information for Baldwin-Felts, but also doing his best to appear a kindred soul to the striking miners during the midst of their conflict. In much the same way Judas dwelt among the disciples, a traitor broke bread among the strikers. But that is where the similarities ended, because, unlike Christ, Sid Hatfield had no knowledge that one of his friends had already sold him out. Moreover, the location of Lively's restaurant, just below the UMWA offices, couldn't have been situated in a better place for a labor spy to acquire critical information. "His place became a rendezvous for strikers, and he was their associate and confidant," penned Howard Lee, in his book, *Bloodletting in Appalachia*. "They repeatedly detailed to him how they planned the slaughter, and described the part each defendant played in it."[1]

For Thomas Felts and Charles E. Lively, the purpose of Baldwin-Felts was no longer just business; it had indeed become personal. There can be no question that Thomas Felts wanted Hatfield dead.[2] The agency's co-owner had seen two of his brothers slain and Lively also lost a brother-in-arms, Albert Felts, who was often the operative's only friend and confidant in his time working undercover out West. Lively now had a new undercover assignment; he was given instructions to befriend the

---

1. Lee, "Bloodletting in Appalachia," p. 62.
2. Any of those who have any remaining doubts about Thomas L. Felts using his Baldwin-Felts detectives in a personal vendetta should know that only a few years before his death, Felts ordered that the agency's records be destroyed. However, most of what is now known about the Matewan Massacre, the trial to follow, and the part Charles E. Lively played in it, came from a box of records which Thomas Felts personally kept in one of his other businesses, and were discovered sometime after his death. Of all the agency's information Thomas Felts could have chosen to retain, these were the only records known to be kept, information regarding the murders and trial of his brothers' assailants, which is available to all at the Eastern Regional Coal Archives in Bluefield, West Virginia.

alleged perpetrators and find information that would lead to the conviction and execution of Sid Hatfield and the others who were responsible for killing the brothers of Thomas Felts.

It was reported in the *Muskogee Times Democrat*: "Felts says he'd like to see Chief of Police Sid Hatfield, who is accused of shooting Albert Felts, 'hanged by the neck.'"[3] In a lengthy statement issued less than a month following the incident, Thomas Felts also castigated John L. Lewis, then-president of the UMWA, and others when he made the following remarks: "The miners and their families living throughout the Western fields, were living in peace and happiness and enjoying as great prosperity as any coal field in the United States; and it was the Bolshevistic teaching of these emissaries which resulted in our men being wantonly and maliciously murdered through one of the foulest plots that ever disgraced a State. Not being satisfied with murder, the helpless bodies of their victims were shot, maltreated, and robbed as they lay on the ground. In their greed for plunder, they even stole the Masonic Shriners' pin from the lapel of my brother's coat."[4]

Although the record would certainly indicate Thomas Felts was a loyal and outstanding detective, he was also a wealthy, Virginia aristocrat, residing in Galax, Virginia. Although Felts was generally hated by the residents of West Virginia, he was equally loved by the residents of Virginia, and was later elected as a state senator. Because of his prominence as a beloved businessman, records show that "three or four thousand people" attended his brothers' funeral in Galax.[5] Records also show, as revealed by Thomas Felts' earlier statement, that he was greatly out of touch with the poverty and hardships faced on a daily basis by those trapped in the West Virginia coalfields. No doubt those beliefs, combined with Felts' lust for vengeance, also fueled his mission to punish anyone who played any part in the death of his two brothers.

Thomas Felts was clearly obsessed with seeing Sid Hatfield punished, so much so that he even followed the smiling sheriff to Huntington, West Virginia, where Hatfield took Jessie Tester-man, the late mayor's wife, to obtain a marriage license, less than two weeks after the violence in Matewan. Upon learning they had obtained a room at the Florentine Hotel, Felts arranged for the local police to bust in on the couple and catch them in bed

3. *Muskogee Times Democrat*, Muskogee, Oklahoma, September 19, 1920.
4. *Roanoke World News*, Roanoke, Virginia, May 29, 1920.
5. *Roanoke World News*, Roanoke, Virginia, May 24, 1920.

together. "On a table beside their bed were the pistols of the dead Felts brothers. They were seized by the police and returned to the Baldwin-Felts Agency."[6] Sid and Jessie were arrested, taken to jail, and charged with "improper relations." Felts, of course, used this occasion to summon his friends in the press, alleging that Hatfield, not his brother Albert, was the one who killed the Mayor. The reason given by Felts is that, on the day of the shooting, the smiling Hatfield had illicit designs on obtaining Testerman's young wife.

Hatfield, who seldom saw any situation as unfit for friendly banter, regaled the local press with his ever-present smile and mountain wit. Sid scoffed at Felts' allegations and explained that the couple had done nothing improper and were unable to locate a minister to make their rendezvous legal. Hatfield said he was only keeping a solemn promise to his friend, Cabell Testerman, that he would look after Jessie if death should ever befall the mayor. "When Hatfield and his fiancée appeared before the local magistrate, he imposed a $10 fine, which would be remitted if the couple married that day. Hatfield submitted his marriage license, dated the day before and His Honor did the honors. Sid and Jessie left town as husband and wife," wrote Robert Shogan in his book, *The Battle of Blair Mountain*.[7]

From the limited number of records that Thomas Felts retained, which are currently housed in the Eastern Regional Coal Archives in Bluefield, West Virginia, it is obvious that Felts employed an intricate system of covert and numbered operatives, such as No. 9, No. 19, and No. 31, all detectives who secretly sent memos back to his agency with information they acquired regarding the killing of the seven agents in Matewan. It is believed these code numbers were issued by Baldwin-Felts to the undercover agents sequentially. "Of the Baldwin-Felts agents, only the identity of 'No. 9' is well-known today."[8] That man was none other than Charles E. Lively.

It is from these memos and through Lively's own public testimony that the public ultimately learned of Number Nine's plans to use the restaurant to infiltrate the close-knit and deadly inner circle of those who participated in the Matewan shootout, which killed two of the Felts brothers and five other detectives. Felts hoped Lively's secretly gathered information might bring

---

6. Lee, "Bloodletting in Appalachia," p. 57.
7. Shogan, "The Battle of Blair Mountain," p. 90.
8. Topper Sherwood, "The Dust Settles, Felts Papers Offer More on Matewan," taken from "The Goldenseal Book of the West Virginia Mine Wars," p. 51.

about Sid Hatfield's conviction and, most importantly to Thomas Felts, Sid's execution.

Moreover, if not for the death of Albert and Lee Felts, it is unlikely the world would have learned of the great majority of Lively's exploits—or to be more accurate—his misdeeds. These preserved intelligence memos chronicle the spy activities of Charles E. Lively; they also provide a greater insight into the character of the man. Operating from his restaurant, Lively's spying and deceit went on for many months, even extending beyond the moment Sid Hatfield and the other defendants went on trial in Williamson, West Virginia, on January 28, 1921. "I remained there," Lively told a reporter, "until about the last of February, 1921, and enjoyed the confidence of Sid Hatfield and others until they discovered by my appearance as a witness in the Williamson trial of the Matewan cases that I was a secret service man."[9]

In order to protect himself should Lively's communications fall into the wrong hands, the detective often spoke of himself in the third person. On September 4, 1920, Lively wrote to his superiors, "Today I was in Lively's Restaurant and overheard a conversation between A.C. Williams and Mrs. Helen Alexander. Mrs. Alexander asked Williams if he thought that they would send him to the pen. He said no, if he had ever though (sic) so he would now be in Canada or other foreign country. He said 'If they do send me, I will always be sorry of one thing and that will be that we ever let any of them get away and if we had took around the block instead of following them, they would not any of them got away at all.'"[10]

The record indicates that Lively didn't lack for confidence in his undercover abilities or in the perceived righteousness of his cause. He also appeared to gloat about the union's clearly unwarranted trust and respect for his aid to the union. His message on June 27, 1920, stated, "Wilson and Doyle both say there isn't an ounce of common sense here, only what Hutchens and Lively uses. Wilson said Lively was the very best man in the field."[11]

In fact, Lively didn't just acquire information related to the killing of the agents in Matewan; he was also complicit in the planning of the miners' future crimes, which ultimately led to

9. *Bluefield Daily Telegraph*, Bluefield, West Virginia, August 6, 1921.
10. Thomas Felts' Papers, Eastern Regional Coal Archives, Bluefield, West Virginia.
11. Ibid.

more future indictments for Sid Hatfield. On August 17, 1920, Lively penned, "It is planned to shoot up Mohawk and Rawl Saturday morning. A few men are to go to Rawl under cover Friday night on the Kentucky side and shoot into the camp, while Allen is to muster every man available to go to Mohawk Friday night on a freight train, get off at War Eagle and split their forces and put some on the West Virginia side. The truck is to be blown up by dynamite as it goes up the hill. Sid Hatfield and Lively are both in on this and I understand that Allen said there would be more ammunition in this week and it would be left with Lively and Sid."[12]

"To show what extent he was in the confidence of the men at Matewan, Lively declared that some of the lunches were packed in his restaurant," the *Bluefield Daily Telegraph* reported, "for the men planning to go to the Mohawk shooting expeditions and plans were discussed freely in his presence, even to the date and almost the hour of the shooting, and the insignia they were to wear. The cayenne pepper which the men purchased and took along with them to use in keeping the bloodhounds from trailing them, was gotten in Lively's restaurant. The pepper and some of the lunches were found on the ground after the shooting was over."[13]

Scarcely five weeks after the Matewan Massacre, Lively's behavior as a loyal union man had persuaded enough people of his solidarity with the union's cause that he was asked to serve as a bodyguard to protect the life of the union's most prominent leaders: Mary Harris "Mother" Jones, Frank Keeney, and Bill Blizzard. Not only was he assigned to protecting the lives of their union leadership, Lively was also tasked with taking the lives of their enemies. On June 29, 1920, Lively reported, "Last night, when Keeney and Mother Jones were going out, Workman saw Mr. Yates and asked me if it was T.L.F [Thomas L. Felts], and said to me, 'Have you a gun' and when I said yes, he said to shoot him dead. Workman, Spivak, A.C. Williams and I guarded Mother Jones against an attack, and Workman and I also waited to protect Keeney and Blizzard."[14] Moreover, since very little occurred in the town of Matewan without the notice of those allied with Sid Hatfield, it is likely that Lively's unlicensed and unlawful carrying of his guns was done with the smiling lawman's full knowledge and consent.

12. Ibid.
13. *Bluefield Daily Telegraph*, Bluefield, West Virginia, August 6, 1921.
14. Thomas Felts' Papers, Eastern Regional Coal Archives, Bluefield, West Virginia.

At the time, Lively had already proven his worth and was now earning a salary of $225 a month from Baldwin-Felts. Apparently, the money was worth enduring the hazards of his work. Lively realized that his subterfuge could place his life at risk, while he betrayed those around him and collected information for the agency. "I was conscious of the fact," Lively said, "that one wrong move on my part and a rifle bullet would ring out and I would be no more."[15]

Lively had good reason to fear what might happen to him should his betrayal ever be discovered by those Hatfield loyalists in Matewan. In August, 1920, Anse Hatfield, the Urias Hotel proprietor who earlier fed and aided the Baldwin-Felts agents, as well as talked to agents seeking to convict those who killed the seven detectives, was assassinated. "Anse Hatfield, victim of the mysterious shooting at Matewan Saturday evening died in a Huntington hospital today... Dr. Edward Simpson, dentist, who was shot at the same time, has a fractured jaw, but is expected to recover. They were sitting in front of the Matewan hotel of which Hatfield was proprietor when shot from ambush."[16] The rifle slug that killed Hatfield "ripped through Anse's chest, came out his back and struck the dentist in the jaw. Both fell."[17]

Lively's investigation also uncovered the man he believed was responsible for the killing of the hotel owner. His memo addressed that issue on September 11, 1920, "I wish to add to my last report, that I heard Sid Hatfield say that Ance Hatfield had to be gotten out of the way. The next morning after the murder of Ance Hatfield, Betty Chambers (sister of Hally Chambers) said it was best news she had heard for a long time, and that she did not see why some of the men did not do it before he got to go before the grand jury." He continued. "It might be well to state again that the night Ance Hatfield was murdered the Sheriff never came about at all. He only lives 1½ blocks from the Urias hotel."[18]

After the seven agents were shot in Matewan, emotions inside the town were running strong and spirited. Among the townsfolk, there were intense feelings of hatred for Chief Sid Hatfield; the same level of venom was also equally reserved for the agents of Baldwin-Felts and those who led them. You can see

15. Hardesty, "Better World," pp. 148, 155.
16. *Bradford Era*, Bradford, Pennsylvania, August 16, 1920.
17. Savage, "Thunder in the Mountains," p. 31.
18. Thomas Felts' Papers, Eastern Regional Coal Archives, Bluefield, West Virginia.

this reflected in Lively's memos as well. On June 8, 1920, Number Nine wrote, "She [Mrs. Cal Houchins] also says that Walden made the statement that the old gray haired S.B., Will Baldwin put a piece in the paper but that it did not amount to anything and nobody believed it, and said that Old Tom Felts would not get off at Matewan."[19] Lively also penned this one on January 30, 1921, not long after the trial began, "There are a good many men, women, and children who are praying that Sid Hatfield will get a death sentence."[20]

The memos even addressed Albert's lapel pin, which Thomas Felts said was missing from his dead brother's coat. Number Nine wrote, on May 28, 1920, "... She [Mrs. Francisco of Keystone, West Virginia] further stated the bodies were not robbed by the murderers, but a woman took A.C.'s tie pin and the money off the bodies..."[21]

Apparently, there were also some earlier discussions with his superiors at Baldwin-Felts, when doubts were expressed about Lively's ability to successfully infiltrate the inner circle in Matewan, particularly in regards to him gaining the full faith and trust of Sid Hatfield, the agency's most hated target. In one of Lively's secret communications, he even appeared to brag to Thomas Felts about his success in effectively worming his way into Sid Hatfield's confidence. On August 28, 1920, Lively stated, "You told me I could not get inside the blood line. Have I not done so?"[22] This daily game of deceit continued for many months, with Lively's wife, Icie, cooking the food and Lively cooking up unsavory schemes for the agency.

It is important to note that any careful reading of these memos makes it clear that Lively's blatant disregard for Sid Hatfield goes far beyond the detective's undercover work for Baldwin-Felts. Like Thomas Felts, Lively's work had indeed become personal.

In another memo compiled by him, Lively stated, "He [Sid Hatfield] lead (sic) a band of Matewanians that terrorized the entire County of Mingo, West Virginia and part of McDowell County, West Va., and Pike County, Kentucky. Many a man I have seen the gang cruelly beat while Sid looked on and laughed with delight although he was Police."[23] Much the same as his

19. Ibid.
20. Ibid.
21. Ibid.
22. Ibid.
23. Ibid.

boss, Thomas Felts, Lively also wasn't going to be fully satisfied until a noose was finally placed around the neck of the ever-smiling, Sid Hatfield.

Thomas L. Felts characterized the miners' unionization efforts as "Bolshevistic teachings," and Charles E. Lively also strongly shared that belief.[24] In a letter to William C. Blizzard, Charles Albert, Lively's own son, said this about his father: "He would sign men up for the union and then turn these men's names over to the Felts Detective Agency when he was in one of his bragging moods. He usually referred to the union men as 'Reds.' And any of them were killed was one less Red to deal with."[25]

It is through these clandestine memos to Baldwin-Felts that the world gains an insight into the mind of Charles E. Lively, Agent Number Nine. Perhaps most enlightening of all were Lively's innermost thoughts, actually revealed in a rare interview the detective granted to a reporter some months later: "My work is my love. When I made friends with Sid Hatfield and his bunch, I put my whole heart and soul in it. My work is chiefly a matter of auto-suggestion. When I talk to and associate with people from whom I want information, or on whom I want to 'get' something, I talk myself into a rock-like conviction that I actually am their friend," Lively explained. "I forget all about being a detective. I clear my mind, my whole conscious self, of every atom of realization of my real identity. Thus, I quickly begin to sympathize with them, earnestly and sincerely, I share their joys and sorrows, I am for them heart and soul. Not until my day—or night, for I do much night work—is all ended and I am alone in my room do I remember that I had an ulterior motive, that I have been 'working.' Then I lock the door, pull down the shade, take my pad and pencil and write my report to headquarters."[26]

From hatchet man to hash slinger, Charles E. Lively's deceptions were exactly what Tom Felts expected from his ace detective. Lively's incidents of subterfuge multiplied in the months to follow. In a set of circumstances nobody could have predicted, the detective's actions in secret soon became public.

24. *Roanoke World News*, Roanoke, Virginia, May 29, 1920.
25. Blizzard, "When Miners March," "Letter by Charles Albert Lively," pp. 386-388.
26. Weyer, *The Cedar Rapids Evening Gazette*, Cedar Rapids, Iowa, August 6, 1921.

CHAPTER 8

Unmasking a Spy

On January 28, 1921, the long-awaited murder trial in Williamson, West Virginia, the Mingo County seat, finally began. There had already been two motions for continuances granted by the judge. Under West Virginia law, a third continuance would have forced the state to dismiss all charges against the defendants. This trial was not a West Virginia legal proceeding as much as it was one man's personal vendetta. Assisting the prosecutor were four lawyers, James Damron, Joseph Sanders, John Marcum, and Captain Samuel Brashear Avis, chief counsel for the Williamson Coal Operators Association, all of them paid for by Thomas Felts.[1] In addition, the trial also had absolutely nothing to do with the killing of the seven Baldwin-Felts detectives on May 19, 1920. Those trials were slated to follow. In the case of this murder trial, Sid Hatfield and twenty-two other defendants were indicted for the murder of only one man, Albert C. Felts.[2]

There can be no doubt that Thomas Felts should never have been permitted to play a role in this state-sanctioned prosecution. Not only was he a private citizen; Felts was also a man with great personal involvement in the case. "Considering that he was brother and employer of the victims, his influence in the prosecution—his apparent ability to subpoena, interrogate, and even relocate witnesses—contradicts modern ideas of blind, impartial justice."[3] Moreover, much of the prosecution's case was built on and directed by the agency's personal investigations of individual citizens, one of them Jessie Hatfield, a woman, unindicted, and in no way, germane to this case.

Felts' legal strategy was designed to assassinate the character of Sid and Jessie Hatfield, who were caught together in Huntington the night before they were married, as if their tryst had been the sole reason for the killing of Albert Felts and Mayor Testerman. Going into the trial, Thomas Felts was

---

1. *Muskogee Times Democrat*, Muskogee, Oklahoma, September 16, 1920.
2. Savage, "Thunder in the Mountains," p. 42. Lee, "Bloodletting in Appalachia," p. 60.
3. Sherwood, "The Dust Settles, Felts Papers Offer More on Matewan," "The Goldenseal Book of the West Virginia Mine Wars," p. 55.

Charles E. Lively on the left. It is believed the man on the right is Thomas L. Felts. The photo is most likely from the period around late 1921, sometime after it first became public that Lively was working for Baldwin-Felts.

(West Virginia State Archives)

obviously convinced that his prosecution strategy would eventually carry the day and lead to Hatfield's conviction. In a four-hour interview with a reporter, Felts said, "'One of Albert's revolvers and a holster were taken off Sid Hatfield at the time I had him arrested at Huntington nine days after the massacre.' Here Tom Felts stopped to produce from his traveling bag a photographic copy of a page from the register of the Florentine Hotel, Huntington, W. Va., dated May 31. Felts pointed to this entry: Sid Hatfield and wife, Matewan, W. Va. 'I guess Sid doesn't know I've got this,' Felts said, clutching the photograph which will be one of the exhibits in the trial."[4]

Felts prepared a harsh and likely slanderous, three-page dossier on Jessie Hatfield: "Jessie Maynard was a lewd woman at a very young age, possibly about the age of fifteen. She was an inmate of a dive at the Hatfield Tunnel, about one mile west of Matewan. She later stayed on a river boat near Black Berry, which was a very tough place, at which place drinking and gambling was freely indulged in. She stayed at Cinder Bottom at Keystone. Trixie refused her admittance to her house of ill-fame because she (Trixie) caught her Frenching a negro in a back alley."[5] The document continued, with a host of other equally-defamatory allegations. It was a strategy which Thomas Felts obviously believed was certain to win the court of public opinion, and therefore would carry over to the courtroom.

The five-page document that the agents of Thomas Felts prepared regarding Sid Hatfield was also filled with similar examples of innuendo and attacks on Sid's character. It began with the following paragraph: "Sid Hatfield. (undisputed) son of Jake Hatfield was born in Pike County, Kentucky, in the year 1893. Jerry Hatfield was the grand-father of Sid Hatfield. Jerry Hatfield's mother was a sister of Old Jim Vance, who was one of the most noted feudalists in the early eighties. Sid Hatfield's mother was a Crabtree and a niece of Old Jim Vance, which made his great-grand-mother and his grand-mother sisters."[6]

The sketch of Hatfield's life also included this bit of information, obviously intended to buttress Felts' contention that Hatfield was a habitual womanizer, who shot the Mayor in order to get the man's wife: "In 1917 J.W. Wilson moved to Black Berry, Kentucky. He was a poor but honest and hard-working

---

4. *East Liverpool Evening Review*, East Liverpool, Ohio, February 8, 1921.
5. Thomas Felts' Papers, Eastern Regional Coal Archives, Bluefield, West Virginia.
6. Ibid.

man. His wife was dead and he had two children, Brack, a boy, and a beautiful daughter about fourteen years of age. Sid payed (sic) court to her while her father was at work, and she became pregnant to Sid. Her father demanded of Sid that he marry her and give a name to the child. This Sid refused to do."[7] The document continued, also including this potentially damning statement: "Sid was noted as a bootlegger and a gambler before he got to be Chief of Police of Matewan. Ance Hatfield claimed to have bought his vote for as little as two dollars."[8]

Other legal and ethical concerns were abundant in this case. Judge James Damron, a prominent counsel member who suddenly resigned his position from the Mingo County circuit court, after passing down the indictments against the Matewan defendants, went to work for Thomas Felts and the prosecution.[9] *The Roanoke World News* reported: "It was in his court that the trials were postponed from September last until this month [January 1921]."[10] The hatred for Judge Damron's actions ran so strong among the miners in the region, he felt the need to request a pistol license from the trial judge, R.D. Bailey, to ensure his own protection.

As the trial date approached, many of the locals could sense that trouble, perhaps even danger, was headed to their community. One newspaper wrote: "There are said to be only two kinds of opinion in Mingo county. One is that the coal operators are in the right and the other is in sympathy with the miners. No one is neutral."[11] In many instances, parents stayed at home and kept their children inside as fear blanketed the city. "The evening before the trial was to begin, fifty picked and heavily armed State Police moved into the city. The following morning, they took up advantageous positions in and around the courthouse. The same morning two score of the toughest of the Baldwin-Felts mine guards, loaded down with guns, suddenly appeared and lounged here and there about the streets, alert and expecting trouble."[12] If that wasn't already enough to strike fear in the heart of Williamson's residents, a couple of days later, it was learned that there were approximately 1,000 union miners forming to come into town and oppose the assembled Baldwin-Felts agents, who they often referred to as "thugs." Fearing that

---

7. Ibid.
8. Ibid.
9. Shogan, "The Battle of Blair Mountain," p. 25.
10. *Roanoke World News*, Roanoke, Virginia, January 29, 1921.
11. *Leadville Herald Democrat*, Leadville, Colorado, September 30, 1920.
12. Lee, "Bloodletting in Appalachia," p. 59.

the tension would eventually lead to violence, the judge summoned the leaders of all parties to meet with him. "A truce was arranged. The mine guards left town, the miners returned to their homes, and the trial proceeded."[13]

If the residents of the town were truly frightened by the prospects of violence surrounding the trial, it wasn't obvious by the way they swarmed to the proceedings. The courtroom was packed daily. The people continued to flock to the meeting, even after Judge Bailey ordered night sessions to expedite turning over the case to the jury. "The novelty of a night session apparently appealed to the residents of Williamson, for the courtroom was soon packed to capacity and many could not gain admission."[14]

On the first day of the trial, while the other defendants were arrayed in overalls and corduroy, Sid Hatfield, the newly elected constable of Mingo County's Magnolia District, entered the courtroom in a brand-new brown suit, recently purchased. His wife, Jessie, wearing pearls, accompanied him.[15] Hatfield's manner of dress, however, wasn't the only thing which caught the attention of those arrayed in the courtroom for the trial. Thomas Felts, Hatfield's primary nemesis, noted a pair of bulges in Hatfield's pockets and immediately informed Judge Bailey that the constable was armed. From that moment, all entrants to the courtroom were searched daily by the deputies.

Unlike some of the reporters on the scene that day, Felts was in no way distracted by the actions of the smiling constable. Felts attacked his manhood and sense of courage. "Sid Hatfield is not that kind of a man," he told reporters. "He showed it in court the other day when he shifted his gun in an ostentatious, threatening way and danced around me, tantalizing me whose two brothers, he is accused of having killed. Were I of a nervous temperament, I would have shot Sid Hatfield down on the spot right there in the courtroom. I had every provocation in the world—and there was a minute when one ever so slight a move on his part would have sent him where my brothers are."[16]

On the first day of the trial, the judge also ordered the bonds to be suspended for the Matewan defendants. Instead of going home at the end of the day, Hatfield and the others were incarcerated in a small jail, which sat behind the courtroom, a

13. Ibid, p. 60.
14. *Bluefield Daily Telegraph*, Bluefield, West Virginia, February 16, 1921.
15. Savage, "Thunder in the Mountains," p. 215.
16. Weyer, *Roanoke World News*, Roanoke, Virginia, January 29, 1921.

situation that did little to dampen the spirits of those on trial. "The wife of the jailer took Jessie Hatfield into her home, so the bride could be close to her new husband. The jailer brought in new mattresses and allowed the defendants to go back and forth between each other's cells, while they played dominoes and visited with their families."[17] Speaking to reporters through the bars of his cell, Sid smiled and said, "This ain't a jail. This is the Matewan Hotel."[18]

The attorneys for both the prosecution and defense had a difficult time in seating a jury, struggling to identify jurors who were in no way related to any of the twenty-three defendants. Over four hundred potential jurors were questioned for their competency and impartiality to man the jurors' box. It was even briefly considered to also place blacks and women on the jury.[19] Although women had recently won the right to vote, the West Virginia attorney general forbade women to serve as jurors; Judge R.D. Bailey obviously quashed the idea of including blacks on the jury as well. One potential juror, who was a cousin of professional boxer and Heavyweight Champion, Jack Dempsey, petitioned Judge Bailey to be excused, because his family contracted small pox.[20] "Finally, on February 9, twelve men sat in the jury box: two school teachers, four farmers, five laborers and an illiterate old backwoodsman who had ridden to town on horseback," wrote Lon Savage in his book, *Thunder in the Mountains.*[21]

If the courtroom spectators were expecting humility on Sid Hatfield's part, or that he might somehow throw himself on the mercy of the court, they were greatly disappointed. With Hatfield risking a hangman's noose if found guilty, the constable still chose to grant an exclusive interview, in which he was asked about the trial. Hatfield said, "'It means no more to me than taking a chaw of tobacco,' he said. 'They can't do nothing to me, nor to any of us.'"[22] As the interview continued, Hatfield came out swinging, answering all the questions with the young lawman's typical smile and swagger. "They shot a hole through my hat and they shot one of my guns out of my hand," Sid said, "I reckon they all was excited."[23] When asked how many of the

17. Shogan, "The Battle of Blair Mountain," p. 93.
18. Savage, "Thunder in the Mountains," p. 44.
19. Ibid, p. 44.
20. *East Liverpool Evening Review*, East Liverpool, Ohio, February 8, 1921.
21. Savage, Lon, "Thunder in the Mountains," p. 44.
22. Weyer, *Logansport Pharos Tribune*, Logansport, Indiana, January 29, 1921.
23. *Fort Wayne Journal Gazette*, Fort Wayne, Indiana, August 21, 1921.

detectives he killed, Hatfield replied, "I don't care if I get credit for all of them—I saw nobody else on my side using a gun. But I did it in self-defense. It was a question of seconds—every fraction of every second meant life or death. It was my life or theirs. I would do it all over again if the circumstances were the same. I could do nothing else. I did no more than any other red-blooded American would have done in my place. I had nothing against those men but I wasn't going to be shot down in cold blood—not if I could prevent it—not me, Bud."[24]

Thomas Felts, who granted an interview to the same reporter, took issue with the lawman's claims. "When Sid Hatfield says that my brother—or any of my men, for that matter—fired the first shot, he lies. My brothers, and the men with them, were trapped like rats. 'Battle?' It wasn't a battle. They were shot down in cold blood with never a shadow of a chance to defend themselves. They were men—they fought when they had to fight—like men, on the square." He also accused Hatfield of treachery when Sid joked with his brother, Albert, only moments before the shooting began. "Do you see the cunning deception? This man Sid could fool and jolly with a man and kill him the next moment."[25]

From the outset of the public testimony, it soon became obvious that the truth would never be fully gleaned from what some of the newspapers were calling the 'Trigger Trial.'[26] The lies and shenanigans were presented equally from both sides, the prosecution and the defense each took turns putting their own individual spin on the events which took place that fateful day in Matewan. While the testimony did little to inform the jury as to the actual facts of the case, it certainly did much to entertain the large contingent of spectators, who routinely attended the hearings.

Many years later, when asked about the trial, "Judge Bailey told me," Howard Lee wrote, "that the defense testimony in those trials was a tissue of the most fantastic falsehoods he ever had to listen to during his years on the bench."[27] But the 'fantastic falsehoods' in this case definitely weren't limited to the defense. The prosecution spun some non-sensical yarns of their own. When Detective McDowell appeared on the stand, he was

24. Weyer, *Roanoke World News*, Roanoke, Virginia, January 29, 1921.
25. Weyer, *Xenia Evening Gazette*, Xenia, Ohio, February 8, 1921.
26. *East Liverpool Evening Review*, East Liverpool, Ohio, February 26, 1921;
   Fort Wayne Journal Gazette, Fort Wayne Indiana, August 21, 1921.
27. Lee, "Bloodletting in Appalachia," p. 62.

asked if the detectives forced any sick women from their homes at gunpoint.[28] The prosecution tried to make the case that, at one of the wives' requests, the Baldwin-Felts men eagerly cooperated and aided them in the relocation of their belongings, "in order to oblige some of the women folks who owned the furniture."[29]

In *The Battle of Blair Mountain*, Robert Shogan wrote, "To strengthen its case against Hatfield and his cohorts, the coal operators' lawyers fell back on one of its favored strategies for prosecuting a conspiracy case—getting one of the alleged conspirators to switch sides."[30] They offered $1,000 dollars to any one of the defendants willing to swap sides and provide testimony for the prosecution. In addition, along with the lucrative cash reward they proffered, the prosecution also agreed to drop the charges against the defector, granting him immunity. "The prosecutors found a logical target in Isaac Brewer, who conveniently was related to two of their number, James Damron and James Marcum."[31]

Isaac Brewer's decision to betray Hatfield and provide testimony for the prosecution was a direct result of Lively's persistent and risky efforts to persuade him, a situation he later detailed in an exclusive interview with a reporter. The detective also plied Brewer with some alcohol, earning his trust while still trying to preserve his status as an undercover operative. "I was the first to tell him he was being framed by Sid Hatfield and others among the 23 men originally indicted," Lively said. "It was the hardest job of my life to get him to believe me, to get him to turn State's witness and to keep him all the time from getting on to who I was."[32]

"It took months of painstaking work. He, like the rest of them, was at first suspicious of me," Lively explained. "Gradually he got the habit of coming into my place. I showed him—his likes and dislikes—how he liked his steak, his chops and everything. I gave minute instructions to my cook."[33] Yet despite Lively's best efforts to win the man over, Isaac Brewer was still not persuaded. One of those times, Brewer even became enraged with Lively, almost to the point of getting physical with him. Brewer's harsh reaction came after Lively said, "Ike, there's a

28. *Galveston Tribune*, Galveston, Texas, February 12, 1921.
29. Velke, "The True Story of the Baldwin-Felts Detective Agency," p. 229.
30. Shogan, "The Battle of Blair Mountain," p. 98.
31. Ibid, p. 98.
32. Weyer, *Roanoke World News*, Roanoke, Virginia, March 2, 1921.
33. Ibid.

rope around someone's neck in this case—and you're the man. Sid and some of the other boys are framing you."[34]

In Lively's interview, the former undercover operative explained how he finally turned Brewer into an asset for the State. "'One night Brewer ate in my place and I decided to turn for good. I told him all I knew. Then I said: 'It means your life or theirs. They are going to swear you fired the first shot. Are you going to swear you fired the first shot and be the goat?'

"'He got up and started to go out. I said, 'Come into the kitchen. I've got something nice.' I gave him a drink of white lightening moonshine whiskey and talked. I gave him another and kept talking. Finally, he said, 'Well, what do you want me to do?' We had another drink. Then I said, 'get in touch with one of the State's lawyers and tell them you're ready to tell the straight of it—tell the whole truth. The boys are going to sacrifice you—go and save yourself.' The next thing I knew Isaac Brewer had turned State's witness."[35]

As was customary with the detective, Lively exhibited no shame for his actions in deceiving Brewer. Rather, he appeared to be proud of it. It is clear that Lively also believed the turncoat's testimony would be instrumental in procuring Hatfield's conviction. "Whatever may happen to the defendants, there's one man I've saved from the gallows—Isaac Brewer." [36]

Once on the stand, Isaac Brewer immediately did his best to slip the hangman's rope around the neck of Sid Hatfield, his one-time friend. "Claiming to be in Chambers Hardware store on the afternoon of the battle, Brewer swore that Hatfield whispered to him, just before the first shots were fired, 'Let's kill every damn one of them."[37] He also testified that he saw Hatfield shoot Albert Felts. However, Brewer, who was severely wounded at the outset of the gun battle, could provide no answers as to who was solely responsible for the shooting of Mayor Testerman. That question ultimately became the crux of the case, forcing the prosecution to once again reach deep into its bag of tricks. Fearing that they wouldn't be able to win their murder case against Hatfield, Felts and the prosecution decided to make a strategic gamble, which proved to be a misguided tactic. That decision required them to unmask their agency's most effective

34. Ibid.
35. Ibid.
36. Ibid.
37. Shogan, "The Battle of Blair Mountain," p. 98.

spy. "In addition, Lively was the eyewitness to nothing that mattered in the trial. He had been in Charleston on the day of the shooting, trying to further ingratiate himself with the UMW leaders. All he could impart in the courtroom was hearsay, the stories that the defendants had told him, well after the smoke cleared."[38]

On February 25, 1921, the courtroom went into an uproar as the prosecution called a surprise witness to the stand. "As a climax to a day of startling testimony produced by the state in the Matewan battle trial in circuit court here, the most sensational was reserved for the last witness to tell."[39] When Charles E. Lively's name was called, "there was a craning of necks and a buzz of excitement."[40] At the same time, Lively was finally exposed and his secret life and identity were revealed and laid bare to all those in the room. "The courtroom was fast emptying before Lively went on the stand, but it soon refilled,"[41] the *Bluefield Daily-Telegraph* reported.

Once referred to as "a quiet sort of chap," Lively was obviously a man who often spoke in low tones and was generally difficult to hear.[42] It was a manner of speech that openly manifested itself in Williamson and later in his Senate testimony in Washington. Almost as soon as Lively took the witness stand in Williamson, the prosecuting attorney, S.B. Avis, was urging Lively to speak up, in order that his testimony might be adequately heard by the judge, jury, attorneys, and court stenographer. Thinking it might offer some remedy to the situation, Avis even admonished Lively, the prosecution's surprise witness, for chewing gum in the courtroom. "I don't believe a man," he said, "can talk and chew chewing gum."[43]

Lively explained his situation, how he came to establish a restaurant in Matewan, and highlighted the undercover activities he conducted while living there. "'Why, when I moved to Matewan,' he said, 'I knew no more about a running a restaurant than a hog does about Heaven.'"[44] Once sworn upon the stand, his testimony generally reflected the intelligence he gleaned, often written down in the evening memos he sent back to his superiors at Baldwin-Felts. Lively's testimony detailed what he and

38. Ibid, p. 99.
39. *Bluefield Daily Telegraph*, Bluefield, West Virginia, February 26, 1921.
40. *Bluefield Daily Telegraph*, Bluefield, West Virginia, February 16, 1921.
41. *Bluefield Daily Telegraph*, Bluefield, West Virginia, February 26, 1921.
42. *Bluefield Daily Telegraph*, Bluefield, West Virginia, August 6, 1921.
43. Trial transcript of the murder trial in Williamson, West Virginia, 1921.
44. *Roanoke World News*, Roanoke, Virginia, March 2, 1921.

Thomas Felts believed to be the potentially damning information he acquired on several of the primary defendants, hearsay on such figures as Art Williams, Reece Chambers, Bill Bowman, Fred Burgraff, men who aided Hatfield in the killings of the seven Baldwin-Felts agents.

The undercover detective also stated that the reason Sid Hatfield killed Testerman, in addition to the lust the former Matewan Chief of Police held for the Mayor's wife, was that he [Testerman] was getting "too well lined up with the Baldwin-Felts people."[45] Lively also claimed that Hatfield had spoken of his desire to kill Anse Hatfield, the friend of the Baldwins and proprietor of the Urias Hotel, who was shot and killed in August, before the trial. Lively said Hatfield had stated he would "kill Anse Hatfield, like he would a dog."[46]

During his cross-examination, Lively also detailed how he won the trust of Hatfield and the others in Matewan and persuaded them to share their secrets. "If you mean that I got their confidence by playing strong to be greatly in favor of the organization, in favor of them killing the men that they killed, by me making it appear to them that I was in favor of that, why, that's what I done."[47] When pressed by the defense counsel for clarification of the things he actually said, the detective replied, "Why, I told them it was a good thing they were killed; that they ought to have done it—that they done a good deed—talking along that line."[48]

Putting Charles E. Lively on the stand was like throwing raw meat before a pack of hungry dogs. Hatfield's attorneys immediately pounced on Lively and attacked his credibility. Lively stated that he had "carried a union card for 19 years."[49] He also claimed that he faithfully paid his union dues, a condition which Lively obviously believed was all that his union oath required of him. "The only advantage was that by joining the union I could make a living—by not joining it," he testified, "I could not make a living. I paid very little attention to my union obligation."[50]

Lively was absolutely tone-deaf as to how his guile would be perceived by all those around him. Laughter filled the courtroom

45. *Roanoke World News*, Roanoke, Virginia, February 26, 1921.
46. *Roanoke World News*, Roanoke, Virginia, February 26, 1921.
47. Thomas Felts' Papers, Eastern Regional Coal Archives, Bluefield, West Virginia.
48. Ibid.
49. *Roanoke World News*, Roanoke, Virginia, February 26, 1921.
50. Ibid.

when Lively flippantly made the statement, "I don't think I left the union at all—as far as I know, I am a member in good standing now."[51] It was this standing which came under the greatest scrutiny from the defense attorneys. If Lively's oath to the union meant nothing to him, then how could the oath he swore to tell the truth in court be regarded as any more credible? It was certainly reasonable to doubt the testimony of Lively, this Judas Iscariot living among them, who ultimately betrayed his oath to protect the union and stand by its brotherhood for his thirty pieces of silver, which translated to the then-lucrative salary of $225 a month.

"If I hadn't practiced deceit and falsehood, I believe I would be under the clay today," he said at the trial.[52] After defending his actions on the stand, Lively repeated the information he gleaned from his private discussions and the statements overheard at his restaurant. But unlike Brewer, who could do nothing to substantiate the allegations that Hatfield killed Mayor Testerman because he wanted Jessie, Lively fully closed the loop on that aspect of the prosecution's case. "'I will have her, if I have to wade through hell to get her,' Hatfield added, according to Lively."[53]

When the trial started, Charles E. Lively was thirty-three years old, married with five children. According to the detective's own figures, he had "worked on 125 murder cases growing out of industrial warfare."[54] There are some reports that before Lively was slated to appear as a surprise witness for the prosecution, he abandoned the restaurant and put his family on a train bound for Bluefield, to guarantee their safety. That story appears to be a falsehood. Although it's known that Lively, for fear of reprisals on his own life, never again returned to the town of Matewan, it also appears that the detective selfishly took no actions to remove his own family from harm's way, or to protect those closest to him, ones who might be seen as high-profile targets for retribution.

Charles E. Lively, at that time, was a hated man and he knew it. He made that knowledge abundantly plain in his interview with an International News Correspondent: "'They know me now,' he sneered, 'and they'll raise heaven and hell to get me. I can tell you, that as that story was read, there was not a State in

51. *Athens Messenger*, Athens, Ohio, February 26, 1921.
52. Ibid.
53. *Bluefield Daily Telegraph*, Bluefield, West Virginia, February 26, 1921.
54. Weyer, *Roanoke World News*, Roanoke, Virginia, March 2, 1921.

this Union where there were not some men clinching their fists and cursing threats to get me if it is the last act of their lives. Afraid, huh? You've got to take your chances in this game.'"[55]

Apparently, the swaggering, long-time, Baldwin-Felts operative was willing to let his family take all the chances in his own game. It is also quite possible that this incident is where some of Lively's family problems originated. His son, Charles Albert Lively, in a letter to William C. Blizzard, who was also the son of another famed union figure of the period, detailed how his father left them to fend for themselves. When Lively once again boarded the train in Williamson, following the trial, he made no effort to reunite with his family as the train passed through Matewan. Instead, Lively stayed aboard and continued all the way to Bluefield alone. However, despite the bitterness many of those in Matewan held for Lively's betrayal, the townspeople exhibited nothing other than kindness to the hated detective's family. "He did not bother to go back to Matewan for the family," Charles Albert wrote. "The union men came to our home and told my mother that the children and her had nothing to fear from them. Then they helped to load some things on the wagon to take to the train station to be shipped when we left."[56]

Following his surprise testimony, the life of Charles E. Lively was never again the same. That fateful day in Matewan, Lively lost a friend in Albert Felts. During a trial for the ones who killed Felts, Lively, too, lost his livelihood. "...After all these years of under-cover work," he said, "I was forced at last to reveal my identity,"[57] His secret life had now been made public. Although the detective still continued his employment with Baldwin-Felts, Lively's value in "secret service" work was forever destroyed. The Agency's most valued undercover operative had to be sacrificed in the desperate attempt to win the murder conviction of Sid Hatfield.

This murder trial was also another seminal moment in the life of Charles E. Lively. After his surprise testimony in Williamson, the undercover detective's secret life became the lead headline on newspapers all across the state of West Virginia and also on many other papers across the nation. It immediately brought to mind the 1914 events in Walsenburg. After his killing of Swan Oleen, the news reports spread across the entire state of Colorado that Lively was a "mine owner's detective." But once

---

55. Ibid.
56. Blizzard, "When Miners March," pp. 386, 387.
57. Weyer, *Roanoke World News*, Roanoke, Virginia, March 2, 1921.

that knowledge became public, there was no place of refuge for the detective to hide, no place in Colorado outside the protection of corporate sheriff, Jefferson Farr, where Lively might truly be safe. The same thing happened in West Virginia when it was revealed to every coal community statewide that Lively was a Baldwin-Felts detective. In every tiny village or hamlet, anyplace where coal was mined in West Virginia, and among all the striking miners and their families, Charles E. Lively was a pariah. He was also a likely target for elimination.

The trial of Sid Hatfield and the others lasted for forty-six days, and included a courtroom visit to the scene of the shootout. There were a number of delays during the trial, with two of the defendants becoming ill, a condition which threatened to create a mistrial. William Bowman contracted influenza and was seriously ill; Charles Kaiser also became inflicted with an unknown ailment.[58] The two men returned to the courtroom and the trial resumed. Although they may have played a significant role in the killing of the seven agents, a number of the defendants were soon weeded out from prosecution when it became obvious that they couldn't have directly taken part in the death of Albert Felts. The closing statements of both sides were often long, deliberate, and occasionally touched with moments of great eloquence. Defense attorney, Harold Houston said, "It is time that Mingo county should be governed by the taxpayers, and not by a private detective agency."[59] He later stated, "But the ways of peace are not the ways of detective agencies or labor spies."[60] When Houston talked about children weeping over the loss of their fathers, it is claimed that "women in the audience cried, and a tear flowed down Sid's cheek."[61]

When challenging Houston's remark about families weeping, prosecuting attorney John Marcum said, "No doubt there were women and children waiting and longing for their husbands and fathers, but they were in the homes of Ferguson, Boorher and Powell, Higgins and the other detectives killed at Matewan."[62]

The defense attorney, J.J. Conniff remarked, "It's ridiculous to believe that Sid killed Testerman because he married the mayor's widow two weeks after his death. Would Sid have gone out alone and precipitated a fight with thirteen men, armed to

58. *Burlington Daily Hawk Eye Gazette*, Burlington, Iowa, February 22, 1921.
59. *Charleston Daily Mail*, Charleston, West Virginia, March 18, 1921.
60. Ibid.
61. Savage, "Thunder in the Mountains," p. 47.
62. Ibid, p. 47.

the teeth, merely to gain his prize? Thank God there's one place the Baldwin-Felts Detective Agency cannot get into, and that's the jury box. They can't get there."[63]

Joseph Sanders delivered the final summation of the prosecution's case to the jury, a presentation that took four hours to complete.[64] Once Sanders was finished, Judge Bailey addressed the jury. "It was dinnertime Saturday, March 19, ten months to the day from the Matewan shoot-out, when Sanders finished and Judge Bailey gave his instructions to members of the jury."[65] The jurors deliberated briefly on Saturday night and took the day off on Sunday. They resumed their deliberations on Monday, returning with an acquittal by lunch.[66]

Upon learning the verdict, Thomas Felts was devastated by the news. "Tom Felts, dreaded by the outlaw world from coast to coast as the most relentless man hunter, who has sent more crooks—bank robbers, highwaymen, feudists—to the penitentiary than any other individual in the United States, never tried to hide the fact that since the Matewan tragedy his whole life revolved around one all overshadowing desire—to bring Sid Hatfield to justice."[67] In this rare and high-profile occurrence, the ever-powerful Baldwin-Felts failed to get their man.

"A few minutes after the acquittal...the writer saw Felts in the latter's [Felts'] hotel room. He lay in his bed writhing in pain, threatened with pneumonia. He raised himself with difficulty on one elbow and said, amid half suppressed sobs: 'We lost. But we are coming back. No conviction of these men seems possible in bloody Mingo. We shall have them tried in another county, and'—his clenched fist pounded the side of the bed with each word—'we shall convict them the next time.' Then he sank back on his pillow and turned to the wall to hide his tears."[68] Thomas Felts was correct; he would be back. Although this first prosecution involved only the murder of his brother, Albert C. Felts, there were several trials yet to be conducted involving the killings of the other Baldwin-Felts detectives. Only two Massacre trials, however, were ever heard by a jury.[69] The second was later dropped by the prosecutors, due to the sudden and violent deaths of two of the alleged perpetrators.

63. *Bluefield Daily Telegraph*, Bluefield, West Virginia, March 20, 1921.
64. Shogan, "The Battle of Blair Mountain," p. 107.
65. Ibid.
66. Ibid.
67. *Fort Wayne Journal Gazette*, Fort Wayne, Indiana, August 21, 1921.
68. Ibid.
69. Lee, "Bloodletting in Appalachia," pp. 63, 64.

Upon their return to Matewan, Sid Hatfield and the other defendants were greeted like conquering heroes. A vast throng of well-wishers were waiting for Sid and Jessie at the Matewan train depot. It took them almost an hour to make their way through a gauntlet of greeters, leaving Sid's hand swollen from the experience. Hatfield was heard to say, "It is good to know you have so many friends."[70] But for Sid, the drama was not yet finished. There were still numerous legal hurdles yet to be confronted. Moreover, for Sid Hatfield and Charles E. Lively, this one murder trial was not the end of their difficulties. They were yet to be reunited in another hearing, this time in Washington D.C. These two, bitter adversaries were both called to testify before a senatorial committee regarding the violence in the West Virginia coal fields.

"Aroused by a description of methods used by private detectives in obtaining information about activities of union miners, Senator McKellar, Democrat, Tennessee, at Washington's hearing before the committee investigating disorders in the Mingo, W. Va., field, declared it was not 'right' for men to work themselves into the confidence of union officials and then to report to detective agencies on what was transpiring."[71] Hatfield and Lively traveled to Washington in July, 1921, and submitted to exhaustive questioning regarding their activities, involving the miners' unionization efforts and those seeking to oppose them. It might also be stated that a great majority of what is currently known about Charles E. Lively, Sid Hatfield, and the rancor that existed between them, was derived from these two hearings, the murder trial in Williamson and the senatorial hearings in Washington.

Less than two weeks after Charles E. Lively and Sid Hatfield appeared in Washington before these senators and testified in their hearings about violence in the West Virginia coal fields, one of these individuals would shoot and kill the other one, in broad daylight, on the courthouse steps of a prominent West Virginia hall of justice.

---

70. Shogan, "The Battle of Blair Mountain," p. 108.
71. *Ogden Standard-Examiner*, Ogden, Utah, July 21, 1921.

Chapter 9

Lively vs. Hatfield, The Final Dance

Although Sid Hatfield was acquitted by the court, Thomas Felts' vendetta against him remained unabated. "Sid Hatfield has been made a hero," Felts said, "by the newspaper and friends—I did not and do not propose to aid that sort of hero worship."[1] The events of August 1, 1921, make it obvious that Felts was not convinced that he would ever achieve any satisfactory retribution from the courts. After all, his agency had a reputation to maintain. "Their slogan was: 'Nobody ever killed a Baldwin-Felts man and lived very long to brag about it.'"[2] Thomas Felts once told a reporter, "My whole life has been devoted to helping the law by hunting down criminals; I am not going to take the law into my own hands now."[3]

Although no conclusive proof has been found that the leadership of the Baldwin-Felts Detective Agency planned and executed a conspiracy to shoot down the killers of Albert and Lee Felts, the circumstances and evidence strain all sense of credulity to think otherwise. "The killing of his two brothers made a broken, embittered man of Tom Felts. It robbed him of his best pals, with whom he had worked and played for nearly half a century."[4] It is certainly understandable that Felts might want some payback. The presence of Charles E. Lively, along with several other Baldwin-Felts detectives, none of whom had any other reason to be there, lounging around the McDowell Courthouse lawn that August morning suggests that Felts, despite any of his earlier claims to the contrary, had other plans to bring his brothers' killer a final reckoning. From his various public statements, it is apparent that Felts determined that Sid Hatfield must face retribution, if not through the courts, then by other more straightforward means. Felts might have claimed that he wouldn't take the law into his own hands, but he certainly had no qualms about putting the gun into the hands of a surrogate, or better still, several of them. Then there is the statement of Charles Albert Lively, the undercover operative's

1. *Roanoke World News*, Roanoke, Virginia, January 29, 1921
2. Lee, "Bloodletting in Appalachia," p. 65.
3. *Fort Wayne Journal Gazette*, Fort Wayne, Indiana, August 21, 1921
4. Ibid.

own son, who wrote the following about his father: "He had allso (sic) stated when Albert and Lee were killed, Hatfield signed his death warrant."[5]

Since Sid was still in Washington, testifying before the senatorial committee, he was shocked to learn about his indictment for "shooting up" the mining encampment at Mohawk, West Virginia. Damning information supplied to the appropriate authorities by Charles E. Lively led to Sid being charged. Despite the newly-elected, Magnolia District constable's ever-present smile, he also held a dark sense of foreboding about the danger he faced in regards to answering these newest indictments.

Before he boarded the train in Washington to return home, Sid told his friend, Fred Mooney, the following words: "Well, old boy, I will never see you again. Felts knows that I have not been in that county and he framed this indictment to get me up there where they can kill me and Ed."[6] Hatfield was not alone in the concerns for his well-being while in the city of Welch. *The United Mine Workers Journal* wrote: "The killing or beating up of union miners is the most popular of all sports in McDowell county."[7] UMW District 17 President Frank Keeney appealed to the governor to take measures to guarantee Sid's safety. Those appeals were rejected. Sid's attorney, Sam Montgomery wrote to one of the state's largest newspapers, expressing his fears that Sid would be killed while facing charges in McDowell County, fears which proved to be fully justified.

Upon returning home from Washington, and as July drew to a close, the McDowell County Sheriff, Bill Hatfield—no relation to Sid—and the Welch police chief, Harry Chafin, came to Matewan, arrested Sid, and took him into custody. The next day, Jessie Hatfield posted bail for her husband and was pleased to learn that Sid hadn't already been killed by his enemies there. In Robert Shogan's book, *The Battle of Blair Mountain*, he wrote, "Sheriff Hatfield promised the wife of his prisoner that her husband would be safe when he returned for the trial, and offered the same assurance to reporters who called. 'There isn't going to be any trouble,' the sheriff told one and all. 'We'll see to that.'"[8] Sheriff Hatfield and his family weren't in Welch the day

5. Blizzard, "When Miners March," p. 387.
6. Mooney, "Struggle in the Coal Fields," p. 87.
7. "Sid Hatfield Killed by Gunmen on the Steps of the McDowell County Courthouse in Welch, W. Va.," *United Mine Workers Journal*, Volume XXXII, No. 16.
8. Shogan, "The Battle of Blair Mountain," p. 155.

Sid returned to McDowell County; however, this very same county lawman had conveniently chosen that same inopportune time to travel to Virginia's Craig Healing Springs, to "take the waters."[9] Sid Hatfield was obviously unaware of the Sheriff's absence. Sid was entering a community fraught with danger, and the only lawman who guaranteed his safety was enjoying a lavish vacation—a vacation which may have been purchased at the generosity of Thomas L. Felts.

Welch, West Virginia, was a vibrant and growing city, with a population of over 3,000, but teeming with political corruption. It was not the sort of place any outsider, with no obvious political clout, could count on receiving a fair verdict. After Welch Mayor J.H. Whitt had been accused of some scandals and improprieties during his term in office, the town council secretly met to hear the charges and consider his impeachment. It isn't clear what the allegations were, but it appears that the matter somehow involved two girls. Upon learning of the council's secret gathering, Mayor Whitt burst through the closed doors and demanded to know the purpose behind their deliberations. Upon learning the reason, Whitt overturned their meeting table and stormed out of the council meeting.[10]

Tasked with the investigation of the mayor was Sheriff's Deputy William J. Tabor, who had been a standout football and basketball player at West Virginia University, along with being wounded and serving with honor in World War I. Although it is unclear if the two girls were included in the earlier meeting, they were being driven to Kimball, West Virginia, that same day, by Deputy Tabor. The mayor pursued and overtook them in his own automobile and ordered the deputy to return the girls to his charge. Tabor offered no resistance, but instead followed Whitt's vehicle back to the mayor's home in Welch. Upon arrival, Tabor pulled ahead of the mayor's automobile and walked back to briefly speak to him. Whitt ordered the deputy to halt, produced a gun, and fired a pair of shots at Tabor, striking the young officer twice.[11] The wounds were not believed to be life-threatening at first. It was later learned that the slugs pierced the 28-year old deputy's thigh and bladder.[12] Deputy William Tabor died the next day. Mayor Whitt was rearrested and tried for

9. Green, "The Devil is Here in These Hills," p. 245.
10. *Bluefield Daily Telegraph*, Bluefield, West Virginia, March 4, 1921.
11. Ibid.
12. West Virginia Department of Health, Division of Vital Statistics.

murder, but acquitted of the charge after only one ballot was held by the jurors.[13]

In June, about four weeks after Mayor J.H. Whitt was acquitted for the murder of Deputy Tabor, he entered the Elwood Hotel in Welch and was confronted by Tipton Carter, a local barber and leading citizen. An argument soon ensued between the man and the mayor. The altercation was believed to be related to simmering marital difficulties between Carter and his recent wife, the former Grace Tresnell, trouble for which Carter claimed Whitt "to have played an important part."[14] Carter pulled a gun on Whitt and began firing, hitting the mayor in the ear and the chest. One of those shots, probably the slug striking the mayor's ear, inflicted a minor wound on a nearby witness. Mayor Whitt charged at his assailant, and the two men became entangled, went to the floor, and wrestled for possession of the weapon. During their struggle, Whitt gained control of the gun. He fired several times, emptying the gun, and mortally wounding Tip Carter in the neck and abdomen. Mayor Whitt fled the city later that same year. This was Welch, West Virginia, in 1921.

On that fateful day in Sid's life, August 1, 1921, Sid and Jessie arose while it was still dark. They dressed and caught the 5:15 train from Norfolk and Western, which took them from Matewan to Welch. Also accompanying them on this journey were Ed and Sallie Chambers, along with Hatfield's friend and, Mingo County deputy, Jim Kirkpatrick. All three of the men were armed when they boarded the train. At approximately 8:00 AM, their train stopped in Iaeger, where Charles E. Lively boarded the train. Lively spoke briefly to the Hatfield party and selected a seat next to Kirkpatrick. Sid Hatfield and Charles E. Lively, these two mortal enemies, both armed and dangerous, rode peaceably together all the way to their destination of Welch, West Virginia.[15]

According to testimony, when they arrived in town, Lively trailed them throughout much of the morning. Unable to get a room, the Hatfield party left their belongings in lawyer, C.J. Van Fleet's room. The Baldwin-Felts agent followed them to the restaurant and ate his breakfast where they were eating. When Sid left the others and went to get a shave, Lively even followed him to the barber shop.[16] Kirkpatrick later looked out the

13. *Bluefield Daily Telegraph*, Bluefield, West Virginia, May 22, 1921.
14. *Bluefield Daily Telegraph*, Bluefield, West Virginia, June 19, 1921.
15. Shogan, "The Battle of Blair Mountain," p. 156
16. *Bluefield Daily Telegraph*, Bluefield, West Virginia, August 4, 1921.

window of the hotel, saw Lively lurking on the courthouse lawn, and stated, "There is Mr. Lively. He is keeping pretty close track of us this morning, isn't he?"[17] Sid looked out the window at Lively, but didn't say anything regarding the spy's presence there. After some discussion about whether or not they should take their weapons, the men decided to leave their guns in the hotel room. At 10:30, the train whistle blew. Carrying the larger gun, he borrowed earlier from Sid, only Deputy Kirkpatrick was armed.[18] Sid Hatfield and Ed Chambers, accompanied by their wives, started their short walk to the stately, granite courthouse, to keep their brief but final appointment with destiny.

In his book, *Bloodletting in Appalachia*, former West Virginia Attorney General Howard Lee wrote: "On the courthouse lawn a deadly reception committee of Baldwin-Felts mine guards, all McDowell County deputy sheriffs and sworn to preserve the peace, was in line to receive the visitors. This committee was headed by Buster Pence, Bill Salter, and Everett Lively—a trio of deadly gunmen. Flanking them on either side were a half dozen other mine guards, all heavily armed and equally deadly."[19] True to Thomas Felts' mode of operation, "The Baldwin Guard System," these detectives had previously been commissioned as deputy sheriffs, but were paid by Baldwin-Felts, also giving Felts plausible deniability as to their relationship to his agency. The men who waited to kill Hatfield and Chambers were all long-time associates of Thomas Felts and William Baldwin.[20]

There remains little doubt they were all hand-picked for this act of extreme retribution. They were tough, loyal, and ruthless agents, men who weren't afraid to get their hands dirty in carrying out an assignment. They were also agents who had no compunction about roughing up a suspect, busting a man's head with their pistols, or leaving their targets bloody or dead, if the situation or their bosses called for it.

Although the agency later denied any affiliation with him, Buster Pence's association with Baldwin-Felts dated back to at least 1910, when William Baldwin, Thomas Felts, and Pence, all jointly petitioned the court for pistol licenses, as special officers

17. Hardesty, "Better World," p. 239.
18. Ibid, pp. 239-246.
19. Lee, "Bloodletting in Appalachia," p. 67.
20. Velke, "The True Story of the Baldwin-Felts Detective Agency," p. 231.
   "Mingo County Operators Admit That They Pay the Salaries of Gunmen Serving as Deputy Sheriffs," United Mine Workers Journal, pg. 10.

for Norfolk and Western.[21] Pence was also well-known "for the tactic he used to escape prosecution for killing union men: 'Shoot 'em with one hand and hand 'em another one,' was the way Pence put it." Planting a gun in a dead man's hand made Pence's self-defense claims appear much more credible when facing investigation.[22] In his time with the agency, Pence had raided bootlegging rings in 1917 and was shot in the finger by a "colored" suspect, Will Jackson, when he arrested the man on a train in 1915. Another Baldwin-Felts agent, Hughey Lucas, lurked near the top of the steps when the shooting started.[23] Lucas, a tall man with brown hair and blue eyes, was later identified as Agent Number Thirteen with Baldwin-Felts.[24] In his book, *The Carroll County Courthouse Tragedy*, Ronald Hall wrote this about Hughey Lucas: "He carried the name of being the toughest man in West Virginia, and Thomas Felts relied on him heavily."[25]

Lucas had been a trusted agent with Baldwin-Felts since 1912, when he took a leading and active role in the arrest and capture of the Allen family, for their March courthouse shooting in Carroll County, Virginia. He also gave testimony, along with Thomas Felts, in the arrest and conviction of Karl Hall for patricide in October 1917.[26] In addition, the detective's relationship with Baldwin-Felts was so intimate, Hughey's youngest child, born precisely the same day Charles E. Lively offered Senate testimony in Washington, was named Thomas Felts Lucas.

William Salter's history with Baldwin-Felts is certainly less documented, although it is known, while working for the agency, he participated in the discovery of an illegal moonshine still in April, 1920, along with being one of the rare survivors of the shootout in May of 1920.[27] It must also be stated that Albert

21. *Bluefield Daily Telegraph*, Bluefield, West Virginia, August 2, 1921.; *Bluefield Daily Telegraph*, Bluefield, West Virginia, April 22, 1910.
22. Shogan, "The Battle of Blair Mountain,." p. 157. Former West Virginia Attorney General Howard Lee, who knew Buster Pence personally, wrote this in his book, "Bloodletting in Appalachia," p. 191: "His stratagem simply meant that he [Pence] put a recently fired pistol in the dead hand of his victim, and then claimed that the deceased shot at him first, and he fired only in self-defense.
23. *Bluefield Daily Telegraph*, Bluefield, West Virginia, March 25, 1917.; *Bluefield Daily Telegraph*, Bluefield, West Virginia, May 2, 1915.; *Bluefield Daily Telegraph, Bluefield*, West Virginia, August 2, 1921.
24. Hughey Lucas Bio, Find A Grave, www.findagrave.com, January 12, 2020.
25. Ibid; Ronald Hall, "The Carroll County Courthouse Tragedy."
26. *Bluefield Daily Telegraph*, Bluefield, West Virginia, October 13, 1917.
27. *Bluefield Daily Telegraph*, Bluefield, West Virginia, April 23, 1920.

Felts placed enough trust and confidence in Bill Salter to name him one of the dozen, hand-picked agents, chosen to join him in the distasteful task of evicting miners from their company-owned homes just outside of Matewan, before the Massacre.

Charles E. Lively waited at the top of the stairs, "talking with a colored man," further proof that Lively was a man who remained unusually calm in potentially deadly situations. Buster Pence was cleaning his fingernails with a pocket knife, also a man strangely at ease when waiting for a man he later claimed to be dangerously armed. Bill Salter later claimed he was in the courthouse, but witnesses placed him at the top of the steps, and from Sallie Chamber's own testimony, Salter was looming over Sallie in her husband's final moments alive. It is not fully known what, Agent Hughey Lucas and Robert Day were doing in those final, peaceful moments when the 10:30 train whistle blew, but they were later taken into police custody, along with Lively, Pence, and Salter, indicating they were indeed close at hand when their potential victims approached the courthouse, walking up Wyoming Street.[28]

As Sid started up the steps, he smiled, waved at the crowd, and said, "Hello, Boys."[29] Those were the last words that ever came from his lips. Charles E. Lively, Buster Pence, Bill Salter, and perhaps, others assembled there, sprang upon the pair of Matewan boys, firing their guns as they charged forward upon their two helpless victims. Their furious shooting, and the barrage of slugs coming from their guns, somehow missed the two innocent wives accompanying them, but it did, however, wound a bystander. "Charley Gutherie, colored, was struck by a stray bullet which entered the fleshy part of his thigh."[30] Lively, firing a pair of guns, shot Sid Hatfield first, spinning Hatfield's body around, and knocking him from the grasp of his wife, Jessie, who fled in fear. While Jessie ran to the purported safety of the office of absent Sheriff Bill Hatfield, her husband's nearly-lifeless body tumbled down the stairs, blood streaming onto the concrete sidewalk below. Although the former Matewan police chief died almost instantly, the detectives continued firing shots into his body. At some point during the shooting, Deputy Jim Kirkpatrick, realizing he was facing vastly superior odds, and knowing he could do nothing to save the already-wounded, Hatfield, ducked behind the wall for safety and then raced away in fear. It is also not known what Kirkpatrick did with Hatfield's

28. *Bluefield Daily Telegraph*, Bluefield, West Virginia, August 6, 1921.
29. Hardesty, "Better World," p. 240.
30. *Bluefield Daily Telegraph*, Bluefield, West Virginia, August 2, 1921.

gun, which he carried along with him to the scene of the shooting, after swapping with the smiling constable at the hotel.

As his fellow agents concentrated their efforts on killing Hatfield and Chambers, Hughey Lucas pulled his revolver and emptied the cylinder by firing multiple shots into the blocks of the granite courthouse. "Three of the flattened bullets were found later by Jailor Waldren."[31] This was obviously part of a well-coordinated attempt to persuade others, and also to lend credibility to the agents' future claims of self-defense, by making it appear that these shots came from the guns which were deliberately placed in or near the lifeless hands of Hatfield and Chambers. "About a year later," Howard Lee wrote, "Lucas told me that he emptied his pistol against the courthouse wall."[32]

Almost as soon as Hatfield was hit, the Baldwin-Felts gunmen turned their weapons on Ed Chambers, shooting him multiple times. Chambers fell in a crumbled heap, on his side, with his back still facing the steps. But unlike the Williamson trial, there would be no acquittals when these agents held court. They advanced on his body, continuing to trigger gunshots into both Chambers' and Hatfield's bodies. At the trial, the prosecuting attorney, G.L. Counts, displayed Hatfield's blood-stained clothing, evidence which clearly indicated that numerous shots had been fired into his prostrate body. Also supporting the prosecutor's contention, "Dr. G.H. Camper, the first witness on the stand, said Chambers was shot eight times and Hatfield six."[33]

Unlike Jessie Hatfield, Sallie Chambers refused to leave her husband's side when the shooting started. She followed his wounded body down the steps, begging the detectives to leave him alone. Lively rushed down towards the fallen Chambers as Sallie pleaded with him, "Oh, please, Mr. Lively, don't shoot him any more, you have killed him now."[34] But seeing Chambers was still breathing, Lively placed a gun behind Ed's ear and administered a final, killing shot into his skull, a wound later confirmed by Chambers' death certificate.[35] Broken-hearted and infuriated by the detective's merciless act, Sallie clubbed Lively with her umbrella. Lively pointed the hot barrel of his gun at

31. Ibid.
32. Lee, "Bloodletting in Appalachia," p. 68.
33. *Bluefield Daily Telegraph*, Bluefield, West Virginia, December 18, 1921.
34. Hardesty, "Better World," p. 257.
35. West Virginia Department of Health, Division of Vital Statistics.

Chambers' wife and said, "Oh, don't you hit me with that umbrella again, you dirty devil, or I will shoot you."[36]

With tears falling from her eyes and her husband's blood soiling her clothing, Sallie Chambers glared at her husband's killers and said to Bill Salter, "What did you all do this for? We did not come up here for this." Hers was a question to which Salter replied, "Well, that is all right. We didn't come down to Matewan on the 19th day for this either." Despite her desire to stay with her fallen husband and her futile pleas for someone to check her husband's body to prove he wasn't armed, the agents sought to usher Sallie Chambers away from the scene. "But there was some men started to run up to me, you know, and those detectives would say, 'Go back, stay back, we will take care of this,' so those men had to stop."[37] As the detectives almost forcefully led her away to the courthouse, where she was reunited with Jessie Hatfield, it was then that Sallie Chambers clubbed Charles E. Lively again, who, this time, jerked away her umbrella and threw it over the hill. Then the women were taken to the hotel, "assisted by several parties."[38] Sallie also testified that after they were returned to the hotel, Bill Salter stood watch outside their door, making it difficult and fearful for her to leave.[39] With nobody friendly to the victims remaining back at the courthouse steps, those surrounding the bodies, all wearing badges and duly commissioned to uphold the law, were presumably free to alter the final crime scene, and to coordinate their stories, to bolster their allegations that they shot only in self-defense.

Unlike his mission to kill a man in La Veta, Colorado, Charles E. Lively had no reason to get himself incarcerated and languish behind bars this time. Moreover, there also would be no guilty plea to involuntary manslaughter, because several of the guns were, according to reports, littering the ground around the two victims. Based on Buster Pence's reputation and past practices, there is every reason to believe the long-time Felts' agent, aided the agents' defense by planting guns in or near the hands of their previously unarmed victims. It is also interesting to note that Chief of Police, Walter Mitchell, who was standing 75-feet away, across the street when the shooting occurred, conveniently testified that "he saw Pence pick up two guns, one beside Chambers' body and the other where Hatfield had been

36. Hardesty, "Better World," p. 258.
37. Ibid, pp. 258, 259.
38. *Bluefield Daily Telegraph*, Bluefield, West Virginia, August 2, 1921.
39. Hardesty, "Better World," pp. 259, 260

standing."[40] It is also quite likely that the gun with six spent cartridges, the one fired by Hughey Lucas into the courthouse wall, was the same revolver, "still warm and containing empty shells, from beside Chambers' body," found by Mitchell.[41] As if to verify that the late, "Two-Gun Sid,' had two guns, the Chief also claimed he found "a .38-calibre two-inch barrel revolver in the right front pocket of Hatfield's trousers and also picked up another .38-calibre revolver by his side. The one in the trousers' pocket had not been fired but there were four empty chambers in the other revolver."[42]

"Thus did C.E. Lively end his 'investigation' of the killing of the Baldwin men at Matewan. He started as a spy, became a judge and jury, and finished as executioner! This is a man that James Damron, erstwhile circuit judge of Mingo County, praised as a fine citizen before the Kenyon investigation committee."[43] When the evening sun sank below the mountains and nightfall loomed upon the turbulent West Virginia city of Welch, Sid Hatfield and Ed Chambers were dead, Albert Felts was avenged, and Thomas Felts and Charles E. Lively tasted revenge. The newspapers of that day also saw fit to point out one additional fact to their readers: "Those who saw the bodies of Hatfield and Chambers after the two men had been shot at the court house entrance positively asserted that the smile of the Matewan ex-chief of police remained even in death. That smile has been the subject dwelt upon by all who came in contact with Hatfield and earned for the him the sobriquet of 'Smiling Sid.'"[44]

Unlike the Matewan shooting, there is little doubt about who the principle assailants in this killing were. Even the spurious and conflicted testimony points to Charles E. Lively and Buster Pence as the main shooters, leaving some questions as to how significant Bill Salter's complicity was in the deaths of Sid Hatfield and Ed Chambers. Although Bill Salter claimed to be in the courthouse, it is known that he was involved at the end, because of the conversation Salter had with Sallie Chambers. However, similar to the Matewan shootout, the deceased in this tragedy largely had no one to speak for them. The testimony of those favorable to the living forever clouded the issue regarding the perspective innocence of the deceased.

40. *Bluefield Daily Telegraph*, Bluefield, West Virginia, December 16, 1921.
41. *Hattiesburg American*, Hattiesburg, Mississippi, August 6, 1921.
42. *Bluefield Daily Telegraph*, Bluefield, West Virginia, August 2, 1921.
43. Blizzard, "When Miners March," p. 143.
44. *Bluefield Daily Telegraph*, Bluefield, West Virginia, August 2, 1921.

There can be little doubt that the seven, fallen Baldwin-Felts agents in Matewan were the victims of vastly, superior numbers. The situation was clearly reversed in Welch, with Baldwin-Felts, or those favorable to them, making up the largest part of the assailants. There is one other fact that must also be stated: unlike the armed men, knowingly-faced by Sid Hatfield in Matewan, however, Charles E. Lively had every reason to believe these two individuals were unarmed and deliberately chose to enter into a situation in which the undercover operative had every reason to believe he would safely prevail. Lively's action on that fateful day makes it clear that he had absolutely no plans to engage in a gunfight; his attack on Hatfield and Chambers was merely an assassination.

The record will also indicate that, by Fall of 1921, Charles E. Lively was responsible for the shooting deaths of no fewer than three men: Swan Oleen, Sid Hatfield, and Ed Chambers, one in La Veta, Colorado, the other two in Welch, West Virginia, respectively. Perhaps there were more dead bodies littering the often-murky pathway of this long-time labor spy. What is known, however, is that there is relatively little proof any of Lively's victims were ever armed at the times of their deaths. There is also another fact which cannot be disputed; Lively was an active agent, fully engaged and employed by the Baldwin-Felts Detectives Agency when Hatfield and Chambers were killed. Moreover, it must be stated that William G. Baldwin and Thomas L. Felts did nothing to remove Lively's badge or sever his employment after the agent's court verdict in 1915, even though the agency's most effective undercover operative had already pleaded guilty to a Colorado charge of involuntary manslaughter. Baldwin-Felts deliberately chose to keep a convicted murderer on their payroll.

Lively had no way of knowing that, after this shooting on the courthouse steps, his life would never be the same. His fortunes were forever altered by this one dynamic and newsworthy event. The story brings to mind the life of Wyatt Earp, who was never able to fully escape the events of October 26, 1881, in Tombstone Arizona. In a similar fashion, Lively was never able to lay to rest his actions on August 1, 1921. In much the same way that every news report or feature on Wyatt Earp inevitably mentioned the walk down Fremont Street and the shooting of the Clantons and McLaurys, nearly every future story on Charles E. Lively referenced his killing of Hatfield and Chambers. Lively's entire life and legacy were forever defined by these few dark moments in Welch, West Virginia, just off Wyoming Street, and he never managed to escape them.

Despite their obvious differences in appearance, one of them always smiling and gregarious, the other somewhat quiet and brooding, Charles E. Lively and William Sidney Hatfield were two very similar men. At the time of their Senate testimony, both men had taken the life of another, yet neither of them appeared to bear any remorse for their individual actions. Moreover, each of them spoke boldly in the justification of their deeds. Although Lively was much less talkative and open about his exploits, he was clearly no less proud of them than Hatfield. Yet when given the chance, Lively was all too happy to hold court with anyone who would listen as he bragged about his killing of Hatfield and Chambers, the ones he said "drew first."[45]

"Whatever may have been the right or wrong in the murder cases, Hatfield himself believed in his heart that he was a great man, a hero, a defender of the townspeople. He was a fanatic on two things—the miners' union and the Baldwin-Felts Detective Agency," a reporter wrote. "Lively, too, is a fanatic. But his fanaticism has little if anything to do with the union or anti-union operations. These things are side issues to him; they happen to figure in the course of his duty: they interest him but little. His one obsession is—his work. He is a detective and wants to be the best detective in the world. Success in his work is his one thought, his one ideal." [46]

The reporter was Siegfried D. Weyer, who wrote extensively about these nearly two years of violence in the West Virginia coalfields. In addition, Weyer also was granted interviews with all of the major players in this drama, such as Sid Hatfield, Thomas Felts, and Charles E. Lively, insightful conversations which, nearly one hundred years later, give the world a much clearer picture of these complex men and the motives behind them. Even today, it is still surprising to see what innermost thoughts he persuaded these often-secretive men to make public.

Weyer also made the proper assessment of Charles E. Lively, who willingly shot and killed two, unarmed men in broad daylight, in public, in direct view of dozens of witnesses. Although Tom Felts was immensely wealthy and had the power to greatly sway high ranking officials and the courts, there were

45. Blizzard, Letter from Lively's son to Bill Blizzard, "When Miners March," pp. 386-389.
46. Weyer, *The Cedar Rapids Evening Gazette*, Cedar Rapids, Iowa, August 6, 1921.

Chapter 9
Lively vs. Hatfield, The Final Dance

103

still no guarantees that Lively wouldn't get the death sentence for his actions or face life behind bars. One wonders what kind of a man would do those things. That behavior certainly doesn't describe a soldier. It sounds more like a zealot. Or, perhaps, those might be the characteristics of a man blindly trying to please someone he saw as a father figure.

The correspondent also made the following statements about Lively: "Men and women are pawns on his chess-board, which is sleuth-work. He is filled with fiery ambition. He will suffer hunger, pain, humiliation—everything—to make good on whatever assignment he gets."[47] Along with that, Weyer added this about Lively, "He is never without his two guns; that he can handle them needs no confirmation here. His gaze is unsteady: he looks at you when you are not looking which may be a matter of training."[48] It is staggering to note the level of dedication, loyalty, and sacrifice--even if it was arguably misplaced--Lively gave to his employer.

Despite the existing rumors that Charles E. Lively had been fired by Baldwin-Felts immediately after the shooting, there is incontrovertible evidence that he was still in communication with the agency and still sending them memos under his alias, No. 9. as late as November 30, 1921.[49] These written communications involved matters which were largely favorable to Lively's own claims of self-defense, or that of others among the agency's courthouse assailants. Regardless of the fact that there is no conclusive evidence that Thomas Felts deliberately conspired to kill Hatfield and Chambers on that August morning, there is overwhelming proof that Baldwin-Felts actively conspired with Lively to make sure that nobody was ever convicted for these two murders. According to James Baldwin, the great grandson of William Baldwin, Thomas Felts came to McDowell County later that same afternoon and plunked down three-thousand dollars cash to bail out the shooters, Lively, Pence, and Salter. Felts posted one-thousand dollars apiece to get these three men out of jail for murder.[50]

"Its secret operatives reported to the Baldwin-Felts Agency that the Massacre was instigated and planned by Reece Chambers, his son Ed, and Chief of Police Hatfield, and the mine

---

47. Ibid.
48. Ibid.
49. Thomas Felts' Papers, Eastern Regional Coal Archives, Bluefield, West Virginia.
50. This information came from the author's personal phone conversations with James Baldwin.

guards decreed that this trio must die. Reece Chambers lived in the narrow valley of the Tug a short distance above Matewan, and his home was within easy rifle range from passenger trains of the Norfolk and Western Railroad. A year after the Massacre, Hughey Lucas, a notorious Baldwin-Felts mine guard told me," Howard Lee wrote, "that for months after the killings, a trusted Baldwin-Felts man and a dead shot, made frequent trips on the train, always occupying a drawing room on the side next to Chambers' house; and that as the train neared the residence, the would-be killer would raise the window a few inches, rest the muzzle of his rifle on the window sill, and peer through the telescopic sight for his intended victims. But danger made the elder Chambers cautious, and he missed death by not venturing from his house when a train was passing. But his son Ed and Sid Hatfield were not so fortunate. Their end is written in blood on the steps of the McDowell County Courthouse."[51]

"Lively stands the avenger of the seven Baldwin-Felts detectives killed in the one-and-one-half minute gun battle at the little mining town of Matewan, May 19, 1920," S.D. Weyer reported. "Among the victims were Albert and Lee Felts. What their brother, Tom Felts, head of the detective agency, failed to achieve with a long and costly trial, for which he had engaged seven of the most brilliant lawyers of the South, the bullets of his 'star sleuth' have done for him."[52]

When sunset fell on the city of Welch, West Virginia, on August 1, 1921, Sid Hatfield was dead. Albert and Lee Felts were avenged; Thomas L. Felts and Charles E. Lively had their revenge. Yet this incident did nothing to quell the violence in the southern West Virginia coal fields. Another flashpoint was soon to follow.

51. Lee, "Bloodletting in Appalachia," p. 63.
52. Weyer, *The Cedar Rapids Evening Gazette*, Cedar Rapids, Iowa, August 6, 1921.

Chapter 9
Lively vs. Hatfield, The Final Dance

105

McDowell County Courthouse in Welch, West Virginia, which looks pretty much the same way it did in 1920.

(JoEllen Yoho)

McDowell County Courthouse, seen from Sid Hatfield's vantage point in the final moments before Lively, Pence, and Salter took his life.

(JoEllen Yoho)

Photo of the author standing in approximately the same place where Sid Hatfield waved to the crowd and said, "Hello, Boys!"

(JoEllen Yoho)

Sid Hatfield's grave, just across the Tug River from Matewan, West Virginia, on a peaceful hillside in Buskirk, Kentucky.

(Author's collection)

Chapter 10

Trial and Aftermath

"While he may not have known it at the time, C.E. Lively set in motion events that would change coal mining and labor relations in the United States forevermore," wrote Gerald Lively—a relative of both Sid and Lively—in his article, Exploitation, Duplicity, Corruption, and Domestic Warfare. "So notorious was the Matewan Massacre and so obvious was the action of vengeance by C.E. Lively on behalf of the coal mine operators, that the federal government could not help but take notice. The light of day was about to shine on West Virginia and all the world would see. But attitudes change slowly."[1]

The burials for Sid Hatfield and Ed Chambers were held on August 4, 1921, a wet and gloomy day in Matewan. Almost three thousand people assembled in the town to watch the activities or to pay their respects to one of their own. Along with the hundreds of mourners, there were also a host of well-armed state police officers to guarantee that order was maintained. The funeral procession went down Mate Street, headed out of the city, the pallbearers carrying the heavy, metal caskets, with each of the widows following behind the individual casket that contained her late husband. They crossed the suspension bridge on the Tug River, into Kentucky, close to where Hatfield was born. "'The strong wire structure swayed and waved beneath the crowds that hurried across in front of the funeral march,' wrote one reporter, and 'it sagged beneath the weight of the caskets as they were born across it one at a time.'"[2] Hatfield was to be buried in Buskirk, Kentucky, near a stream which was known as Blackberry Creek.

"The major part of the people of Matewan swore by Sid Hatfield," S.D. Weyer wrote. "He was their hero. He was known to 'go through Hell' for a friend and was equally intense in his antagonisms. He never forgot and never forgave. He was

---

1. Gerald Lively, *Daily Kos*, "Exploitation, Duplicity, Corruption, and Domestic Warfare—The West Virginia Coal Industry," https://www.dailykos.com/stories/2014/1/18/1270728/-Exploitation-duplicity-corrpution-and-domestic-warfare-the-West-Virginia-coal-industry, December 31. 2019.
2. Green, "The Devil is Here in These Hills," p. 248.

intensely proud in mountaineer fashion. Beneath his grinning, unsophisticated exterior, he hid a world of shrewdness and cunning."[3]

Once the pallbearers slogged through the mud to the hillside cemetery and reached the victims' final resting place, the mourners were treated to an impassioned eulogy, delivered by Hatfield's attorney, Sam Montgomery. He described their killers as "Sleek, dignified church-going gentlemen who would rather pay fabulous sums to their hired gunman to kill and slay men for joining a union than to pay a bit more to the men who delve into the subterranean depths of the earth to produce their wealth for them."[4] The lawyer continued, "There can be no peace in West Virginia until the enforcement of the law is removed from the hands of private detective agencies, and from those deputy sheriffs who are paid, not by the state, but by great corporations, most of them owned by non-residents who have no interest in West Virginia's tomorrow." When the storm clouds let loose and rain poured down upon the crowd, Montgomery said, "Even the heavens weep."[5]

"The UMW closed its headquarters in Charleston and placed a placard on the door that asked a pointed question: 'Shall the government live of the people, for the people and by the people of West Virginia or be destroyed by the Baldwin-Felts detective agency?' In many of the nation's newspapers, the coverage of the funeral overshadowed the news that the unforgettable tenor of Enrico Caruso would be heard no more, the world's most celebrated opera star having died of pneumonia in Naples the day after Hatfield and Chambers were slain.[6] The UMW placard also said, "Closed in memory of Sid Hatfield and Ed Chambers, murdered by Baldwin-Felts detectives while submitting to a court of law."[7]

The killing of Sid Hatfield and Ed Chambers resulted in an onslaught of negative opinion throughout much of the nation. "*The Wheeling Intelligencer* called it 'the most glaring and outrageous expression of contempt for the law that has ever stained the history of West Virginia.' The UMW Journal said, 'Probably never in the history of the country did a cold-blooded

3. Weyer, *The Cedar Rapids Evening Gazette*, Cedar Rapids, Iowa, August 6, 1921.
4. Green, "The Devil is Here in These Hills," p. 248.
5. Savage, "Thunder in the Mountains," p. 73.
6. Shogan, "The Battle of Blair Mountain," p. 160.
7. Savage, "Thunder in the Mountains," p. 74.

murder ever create so much indignation.'"[8] However, *The New York Times*, after fomenting and sensationalizing much of the violence in the earlier Hatfield and McCoy feud, made light of the shooting in an editorial regarding events from that region: "Perhaps the private detective LIVELY acted his name," they wrote. "The good behavior of the crowd of mountaineers deserves a kind word. There was none of that neurotic excitement which would have blazed up in communities of ordinary heredity. It was an orderly, quiet and successful shooting match. That it took place in the shadow of a court house needn't prompt us to any obvious moralizing or special virtuous indignation."[9]

The detectives' actions in Welch also brought another murder trial to the region, one which brought this latest act of West Virginia coal violence more newspaper headlines and greater national prominence. "When Hatfield and Chambers went into Welch, W. Va., they went into an 'unfriendly' county, McDowell, where the Felts men are strong," reported the *Fort Wayne Journal Gazette*. "If it is true, as Tom Felts said, that no jury in Mingo will ever convict the Matewan accused, it is equally safe to say that it will be difficult to find a jury in McDowell county to convict Lively."[10] Those words were indeed prophetic.

Charles E. Lively, like Hatfield before him, while facing a trial which could result in placing a noose around his neck, also chose to grant an interview to a news reporter, a situation he undoubtedly hoped would influence the jury pool. It might also be stated that Lively's description of the incident, and the part he played in the violence, were remarkably similar to those things said earlier by Sid Hatfield about the shooting in Matewan. Perhaps Lively's lawyer advised him on the interview ahead of time, recommending that the detective use language which was strikingly similar to what Hatfield said to the reporter in his own pre-trial interview. Rather than make excuses for the incident, Lively embraced his role, also adding some creative flourishes of his own. "'I regret having had to shoot either of these men,' Lively said, 'but it is a case of self-defense, pure and simple. I knew that if Sid got what he considered a 'good chance' it would be either his life or mine.'"[11]

8. Ibid, p. 74.
9. *The New York Times*, August 3, 1921.
10. *Fort Wayne Journal Gazette*, Fort Wayne, Indiana, August 21, 1921.
11. *Associated Press*, *Washington C.H. Daily Record*, Washington Court House, Ohio, August 6, 1921.

Lively's description of that day at the courthouse continued. "'I happened to look down the steps and there stood Sid Hatfield, Ed Chambers and their wives on the first landing. They were looking at me and exchanged glances, nodding their heads. Sid said something to Ed I couldn't hear. Suddenly they stepped apart. I could see Sid's jaws set like a steel trap. Both men pulled their guns; as they did so I jumped to my feet and pulled mine. Sid fired at me and I immediately shot back. I had two pistols and was using both. Sid staggered and fell, as did Chambers immediately afterwards. Then Mrs. Chambers attacked me with her umbrella. I grabbed the umbrella, threw it away and then walked over to the office of A.C. Hufford, justice of the peace, and surrendered. The report that I shot into Chambers' body while he was lying on the steps dead is an absolute falsehood.'"[12]

The prosecutor, thinking he had the best chance to win a murder conviction in the death of Ed Chambers, brought that case to trial in December of 1921. Indicted for Chambers' murder, Buster Pence, Bill Salter, and Charles E. Lively faced a friendly jury in Welch, a place not hospitable for union organizing. One eyewitness, J.B. Hicks, said Lively started the shooting and identified the three defendants as the ones who did the shooting.[13] "Some of the witnesses were jurors who were waiting for court to reconvene when the firing started and others were men who happened to be in the street at the time. John Lunsford, of Powhatan, one of the jurors at the time, testified that Lively fired the first shot of the pistol battle and that Chambers fell at the second shot."[14] J.W. Sigmund, another juror, also testified that Lively fired first.[15] Yet none of these witnesses proved to be enough to sway the direction of the case.

Fabricated testimony was as frequent in the McDowell County trial as it had been in the Williamson trial. Buster Pence testified first and was very creative with his version of the events. "'I was standing at the top of the steps manicuring my nails when the shooting started,' he said. 'At the first crack of the gun I threw back my head and saw Sid Hatfield and his wife and Ed Chambers and his wife. Sid was shooting and Ed was reaching for his gun. It seemed as if I was looking right down into the barrel of his gun. I dropped my knife in my pocket without

12. *Associated Press, Hattiesburg American*, Hattiesburg, Mississippi, August 6, 1921.
13. *Bluefield Daily Telegraph*, Bluefield, West Virginia, December 14, 1921.
14. Ibid.
15. Ibid.

closing it and drew my pistol and started shooting.'"[16] Not to be outdone by anybody for a lack of candor, Pence later even claimed that "he did not know Lively until after they were in jail and he heard some one call Lively by name."[17]

In regards to Buster Pence's testimony, one has to wonder why Pence just happened to be at the top of the steps on that day when the shooting started. What business did he have to conduct at the courthouse that particular morning? Pence had no part in the Mohawk incident and could provide no testimony on this charge for which Hatfield was indicted. It must also be noted that none of the eyewitnesses stated that Hatfield was allegedly shooting anything other than one gun as he came up the steps. How was that one gun pointed at both Lively and Pence at the same time? Also, what made Buster Pence believe that Sid was shooting at him? If Lively's testimony is to be believed, about Hatfield drawing a gun to target Lively, then that means Pence obviously perjured himself on the stand, when he said the gun was pointed at him, as well.[18]

In addition to those items, the evidence also reveals that Baldwin-Felts deliberately sought to distance themselves from Buster Pence. If the shooting on the courthouse lawn was not truly a conspiracy conceived by Thomas Felts to kill Sid Hatfield, then why did Baldwin-Felts find it necessary to lie about one of their own men afterwards, immediately claiming that Buster Pence had no relationship to them? "In a statement issued from the offices of the agency here last night, it was said George [Buster] Pence was in no way connected with the agency but was a deputy sheriff of McDowell county."[19] That claim is certainly spurious, to say the least, because this work has already documented Pence's extensive relationship to the agency and with Thomas Felts, dating as far back as 1910, along with the arrests Pence made while working for the agency in 1915 and 1917.[20]

"Prosecuting attorney, G.L. Counts, in cross-examining Salters, asked if he was employed by the Baldwin-Felts detective agency, but the witness declared he had not been in the employ

16. *Gettysburg Times*, Gettysburg, Pennsylvania, December 17, 1921.
17. Ibid.
18. See Appendix B.
19. *Bluefield Daily Telegraph*, Bluefield, West Virginia, August 2, 1921.
20. *Bluefield Daily Telegraph*, Bluefield, West Virginia, April 22, 1910.; *Bluefield Daily Telegraph*, Bluefield, West Virginia, May 2, 1915.; *Bluefield Daily Telegraph*, Bluefield, West Virginia, March 25, 1917.

of the agency for the past three years."[21] Salter's testimony was obviously false, since it is known he was one of the rare survivors of the thirteen agents who evicted striking miners from their homes on May 19, 1920, the day of the Matewan Massacre. There is further evidence that Salter was also working for Baldwin-Felts when he discovered a moonshine still in April of the same year.[22] Based on this glaring example of Salter's perjured testimony, his denials to the allegations that he had done any shooting, and Salter's own claims that "he was just coming out of the court house when the shooting started,"[23] also become subject to extreme doubt. In addition, Salter has been identified by the witnesses, and one of the victim's wives, as one of the courthouse assailants.

Upon taking the stand, Charles E. Lively's testimony rarely differed from what he already told the reporter in his earlier interview. "Answering questions by defense attorneys, Lively said he knew Hatfield to be a dangerous man, and had been informed that Hatfield was going to kill him, at the first opportunity."[24] While there remains little doubt that Hatfield was precisely the sort of man who might wish to seek retribution on the one who betrayed him, it is obvious that Matewan's former Chief of Police had numerous opportunities on August 1, 1921, to engage the detective in a more equitable gunfight. However, after passing up those other chances to kill his betrayer, it makes no sense to conclude that Sid Hatfield would also place his young bride's life at risk to shoot it out with Lively on the courthouse steps.

Once again, Lively, while in court, reiterated the phrase that "Sid Hatfield's jaw set like a steel trap," as if the condition of Sid's jaws somehow constituted a direct threat on the detective's life and was provocation for murder.[25] Lively's testimony leaves one to wonder how Sid's jaw was set when Lively boarded the train and chose a seat next to the Hatfield party. How was Sid's jaw fixed when Lively spoke to Ed Chambers at the depot in Welch? And what was the state of Sid's jaw when Lively shadowed them into the restaurant for breakfast? Perhaps Hatfield's jaw was also present when Lively followed him to the barber shop. Of course, Lively also "denied he had seen Hatfield

21. *Bluefield Daily Telegraph*, Bluefield, West Virginia, December 17, 1921.
22. *Bluefield Daily Telegraph*, Bluefield, West Virginia, April 23, 1920.
23. *Bluefield Daily Telegraph*, Bluefield, West Virginia, December 17, 1921.
24. Ibid.
25. Ibid.
26. Ibid.

or Chambers on the train and said he did not see them until the train reached Welch and he had started from the railroad station. He was especially emphatic in his denials that he had followed the Hatfield party."[26] One can certainly understand Lively's harsh denials that he trailed them, because the agent's claims of self-defense, combined with his allegations that Hatfield planned to kill him, are greatly undermined by Lively's multiple interactions with his victims on the day of the courthouse shooting.

One must ask why any of these other meetings between Hatfield and Lively didn't also conclude in a violent and bloody confrontation. The answer is glaringly obvious. Lively may not have been afraid of Smiling Sid, but he also wasn't foolish enough to confront the man directly, either. The detective wisely chose to pass up those other opportunities to enter into a gunfight with Sid Hatfield, because it is reasonable to assume the undercover operative feared that, on these other occasions on August 1st, Sid was fully armed and the odds were not overwhelmingly in Lively's favor. Such was not the case on the McDowell County courthouse steps, where the situation—and the numbers—clearly gave Lively and his fellow agents an upper hand. While it may certainly be true that the cloak-and-dagger lifestyle which Lively chose to live lends some credibility to the I.N.S. reporter's claims that the detective "knows no fear," it must also be stated that there is no palpable evidence that Lively, throughout his life and career, despite killing no fewer than three men, ever personally engaged in a gunfight with an equally-armed individual.[27]

There can be little doubt that Charles E. Lively joined Bill Salter and Buster Pence in deliberately perjuring themselves on the stand. There can also be little doubt that their prevarications worked when presented before a friendly jury in a week-long trial. The three Baldwin-Felts defendants were acquitted of murdering Ed Chambers after the jury deliberated for only "fifty-one minutes." Upon hearing the verdict, the prosecutor asked that the defendants be held for the murder indictments involving the death of Sid Hatfield.[28]

The Bluefield Daily Telegraph reported: "Attorney J.N. Harman, Jr. one of the legal representatives who defended the accused men in the recent trial, stated Saturday night in his

27. Weyer, *The Cedar Rapids Evening Gazette*, Cedar Rapids, Iowa, August 6, 1921.

28. *Bluefield Daily Telegraph*, Bluefield, West Virginia, December 18, 1921.

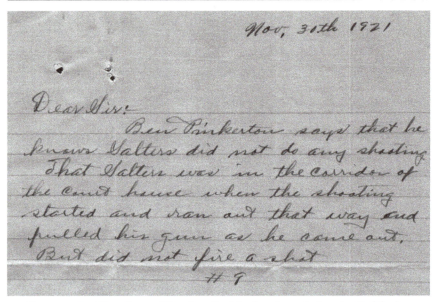

Communication from Charles E. Lively, Agent #9, to Baldwin-Felts, information acquired by Lively to win his acquittal for the courthouse shooting.

(Thomas Felts Collection, Eastern Regional Coal Archives)

opinion the case would never be brought to trial, although it is set for the January term. Mr. Harman based his prediction on the fact the state had selected the Chambers case as the strongest and best hope to secure conviction; that the two cases were practically one and the same; that all the evidence came out in the Chambers case and the jury had quickly decided on an acquittal."[29] Mr. Harman was clearly not wrong in his assertion. Although there was a murder trail conducted in the McDowell County courthouse shooting, absolutely nobody was ever tried for the murder of Sid Hatfield, a significant distinction that certainly wasn't lost on Thomas Felts, who desperately wanted retribution for the killing of his two brothers. Moreover, it must be stated again: nobody ever stood trial for the murder of Sid Hatfield. In addition, it was the Allen family incident, a bloody shooting inside a courthouse that brought Baldwin-Felts their greatest acclaim, but it was an equally-bloody shooting outside a courthouse which brought them their greatest condemnation, and that left an indelible stain upon the name and reputation of Baldwin-Felts as strictly a law enforcement agency.

---

29. Ibid.

The killing of Sid Hatfield may have closed "another chapter in the dark and bloody history of the Mingo County mine disturbances," but it only closed a single chapter.[30] Lively's acquittal merely signaled the beginning of a different chapter, perhaps more ominous than the one before. It has often been said that 'violence begets violence," but never was this statement truer than in the mine wars of West Virginia. In much the same way that the Matewan Massacre led to a daring and brazen assassination on the courthouse lawn, the freeing of Lively was also the flashpoint for a raging inferno by outraged miners throughout the state, culminating in the Battle of Blair Mountain. "On August 7, six days after the murder of Hatfield and Chambers 5,000 coal diggers met in Charleston, ostensibly to present a list of demands to the governor. During the ten-hour meeting, they listened to speeches from Mother Jones, Bill Blizzard, and then Keeney, who reportedly told them, 'You have no recourse except to fight. The only way you can get your rights is with a high-powered rifle, and the man who does not have this equipment is not a good union man.'"[31]

"From the written notes and diaries of coal company spies and coal operators it is evident that there was considerable 'unrest' in the whole Kanawha field from the time of the killing of Hatfield and Chambers on August 1 until the culmination of the miners' anger in the Armed March," wrote William C. Blizzard, in his book, *When Miners March*. "It is significant to observe that these records reveal that standard equipment of every coal company in these peaceful, organized localities seemed to be a large supply of high-powered rifles and an occasional machine gun. Just why they kept such arsenals is not clear, but it was certainly not to hunt the squirrels that abounded in the surrounding hills. The miners knew of the arsenals and simply appropriated them; in many cases, however, promising to return them at a later date. There is every reason to believe that the coal miners, after learning of the refusal of Governor Morgan to listen to their requests of August 7, met in their local unions and made decisions as to their willingness to participate in an Armed March into Logan and Mingo, the assembly point being in Marmet."[32]

With his declaration of martial law in Mingo County, Governor Morgan appointed Major Thomas B. Davis, "chief agent in charge of administering martial law." Often maligned as

30. Ibid.
31. Corbin, "Life, Work, and Rebellion in the Coal Fields," p. 217.
32. Blizzard, "When Miners March," p. 274.

the "Emperor of the Tug River," Davis was a little man who longed for war-time glory, but saw his only action at home.[33] "Although the assassinations at Welch got the miners' blood boiling, the marchers were not simply out for revenge. They had embarked on a mission to free their brothers imprisoned under Major Davis's military regime,"[34] penned James Green in his book, *The Devil is Here in These Hills*. Believing he generally had the power to do whatever he wished, Davis once stated, "The big advantage of this martial law is that if there's an agitator around you can just stick him in jail and keep him there."[35] The District 17 leadership, Frank Keeney and Fred Mooney, led reporters to believe the marchers were not led by any one man, but rather a unified, purposeful, and collective effort, undertaken by the miners themselves. That was clearly not the case. "Twenty-eight-year-old William Blizzard, Keeney's friend from Eskdale on Cabin Creek, had assumed overall command of the army and led it through Boone County, where Blizzard served as subdistrict director of the UMWA."[36]

The armed marchers, nearly 8,000 strong, were often commanded by men who experienced actual combat in the Spanish-American War or World War I. Several of the men wore the uniforms they brought back from overseas. But more often than not, those citizen-miners were meagerly adorned with their blue denim, bib overalls. The marchers identified themselves with their red bandanas, which were an essential part of every miners' gear.[37]

The reason for the red bandanas, according to Wess Harris in his book, *Written in Blood*, is that despite having to "pay for their own tools and supplies, the ever-generous coal companies provided red—and only red—bandanas free of charge."[38] This square piece of cloth was the only item the coal companies gave to the miners; everything else the miners purchased. The red bandana, when placed on a wound, didn't allow blood to show through the fabric. It just appeared wet, which lessened the

33. Shogan, Robert, "The Battle of Blair Mountain." Page 123.
34. Green, "The Devil is Here in These Hills," p. 256.
35. Ibid, p. 231.
36. Ibid, p. 261.
37. One has to wonder if the red sashes—which have no basis in history and were little more than another Hollywood invention—worn by the Cowboys in the 1993 film, Tombstone, may have actually been inspired by the miners' red bandanas, which were uniformly worn to identify themselves to other miners, when the Redneck Army marched on Blair Mountain in 1921.
38. Wess Harris, "Written in Blood: Courage and Corruption in the Appalachian War of Extraction," (PM Press, 2017), p. 97.

chances of a wounded miner going into shock after being injured. The outraged miners proudly wore those red bandanas around their necks as a form of uniform, to identify themselves to each other, which probably originated the term, 'rednecks.'

Although there was nobody around to officially confirm it, newspapers were reporting that the marchers were targeting Logan County, West Virginia. The county was ruled by Sheriff Don Chafin, a man whose personal whims dictated who won local elections and attained power in Logan County. Don Chafin had much in common with Jefferson Farr in their hatred and abuse for striking miners. The same way that Farr was a corporate sheriff in Huerfano County, Colorado, in 1914, Chafin was equally beholden to the coal companies in 1921. "The Logan County coal operators paid Chafin a huge annual salary of $30,000 to act as their guardian; it was a task he performed with the aid of forty-six active deputies. Chafin, who had five hundred more men on the inactive rolls in case they were needed, assigned his men to patrol every rail station in the county to watch for troublemakers and to use whatever means necessary to remove them."[39]

Sheriff Chafin also had no use for the detectives of Baldwin-Felts. It's not that Chafin didn't like them; it's simply that he didn't need them. His campaign promise to eliminate the hated mine guard system may have proven worse than the alterative. In the ongoing battle between miners seeking to unionize and coal companies seeking to stop them, the sheriff determined he wasn't willing to split his ill-gotten gains with anyone from a third party. Chafin's many deputies were all fully capable of handing the pistol-whippings and intimidation themselves.

In a report out of Charleston, it was learned: "Efforts to recruit a large body of former service men to fight union miners marching into Logan county failed here today. A meeting of the American Legion to effect a defense organization was held next door to the executive mansion of Governor Morgan. It broke up with cat calls and jeers for speakers favoring organization and the singing of 'We'll hang Don Chafin to a sour apple tree.'"[40] Knowing that thousands of armed miners were set to invade Logan, Chafin made preparations to defend his realm. "The sheriff then mobilized forty-four of his deputies and opened up the arsenal of weapons he had been stockpiling since the first union invasion threat in 1919," James Green wrote. "The cache

39. Green, "The Devil is Here in These Hills," p. 183.
40. *Santa Ana Register*, Santa Ana, California, September 1, 1921.

included ten machine guns, a thousand rifles, and sixty-seven thousand rounds of ammunition."[41]

Sheriff Chafin wasn't only concerned about having the armaments to defend Logan County; he also needed men. "Every able-bodied man who could be lured, persuaded, bought or coerced into joining Chafin's forces of 'law and order' was mobilized into a small army and marched toward Blair Mountain. We say 'coerced' advisedly, for Chafin's methods of recruiting soldiers were in some cases similar to his methods of combating unionism."[42] Chafin's conscripted army lined the hills, digging trenches and establishing machine gun placements. "Defenders massed their forces at gaps along the ridge, particularly Blair Mountain Gap, a pass between two 1,800-foot peaks that make up Blair Mountain. A dirt road ran through the pass, providing a natural avenue to the town of Logan. But defenders positioned on the crest of the mountain peaks could command the approaches to the pass and the mountain, and make any invading force pay a heavy price."[43]

Despite the miners' overwhelming numbers and their claim to possess the moral high ground, the summits all belonged to Sheriff Chafin. Despite their zeal, the beleaguered miners, armed with their small weapons, ultimately stood no real chance of victory in a simple gun battle. Chafin's army only needed to slow down the Redneck Army until federal troops were ordered to the area. The miners were held at bay by better armaments and superior troop placements. And had a concentrated attack on the mountain been waged by the miners, the casualties would have been massive. But as much as the armed marchers hated corrupt sheriffs, predatory coal companies, and their generously-paid band of corporate enforcers with Baldwin-Felts, the miners were indeed patriots, men who had no interest in taking up arms against Uncle Sam.

Secretary of War John Weeks selected Brigadier General Harry Bandholtz to bring a halt to the violence in West Virginia. "In distinguishing himself in both wars that his country had waged against foreign foes during his lifetime, Bandholtz had displayed a notable combination of soldierly courage and discipline with diplomatic tact and negotiating skill."[44] After sending infantry troops into the region, the general contacted the

41. Green, "The Devil is Here in These Hills," p. 263.
42. Blizzard, "When Miners March," p. 299.
43. Shogan, Robert, "The Battle of Blair Mountain," p. 174
44. Ibid, p. 175.

union leadership, summoned them to the governor's office, and sternly warned them to abandon the fighting. "'You two are the officers of this organization and these are your people,' the general told Mooney and Keeney. 'I am going to give you a chance to save them, and if you cannot turn them back, we are going to snuff this out like that.' For emphasis, he snapped his fingers right in Mooney's face."[45] Keeney and Mooney rushed off to meet with a gathering of the troops. After presenting their case to the Redneck Army, a majority of the miners reluctantly agreed to call off their march and return to their families. General Bandholtz quickly reported the good news to Washington and made his way home.

Although Bandholtz was a superb military general and diplomat who obviously believed everyone involved in this conflict wanted peace to reign in those southern West Virginia coalfields, he couldn't have been more wrong in that belief. Sheriff Don Chafin never wanted peace with the striking miners; Chafin wanted payback. He also desired to see the union crushed forever. As the Redneck Army appeared to be disbanding, returning to their homes, and laying down their arms, Chafin and State Police Captain J.R. Brockus conspired to arrest a few dozen of the miners, those who had detained and disarmed the state policemen earlier in the conflict. The battle could have been over, if not for the pride and wounded ego of Sheriff Chafin. "He sent 200 sheriff's deputies to join the ninety troopers under Brockus's command."[46] Near the town of Sharples, West Virginia, Brockus captured and disarmed several miners, forcing them to walk ahead of his column of state policemen and Chafin deputies. On the road, Brockus encountered several armed miners. With tensions already running high in the region, a gunfight quickly ensued, in which several of the captives were shot and killed. Upon hearing the shooting, other locals grabbed their arms and joined in the battle. With the deputies and state policemen scattering for their lives, Brockus wisely decided to head for the safety of Logan. In the midst of the shooting and confusion, four of the deputies were captured by the miners.

"On Sunday, August 28, news of Brockus's incursion spread rapidly through Southern West Virginia. What had happened was bad enough, but reports of the encounter soon made things seem worse."[47] The accounts of the shooting eventually snowballed, growing larger with each telling, leading to stories of

45. Ibid, p. 177.
46. Ibid, p. 186.
47. Ibid, p. 187.

women and children being slaughtered by Brockus and his gang. Knowing they had already been charged with murder and fearing they might meet the same fate as Sid Hatfield, Keeney and Mooney escaped to Ohio. Their departure put Bill Blizzard solely in charge of this ragtag army, which was now reforming to respond to this latest act of aggression directed against the miners by Chafin and Brockus. The truce, which General Bandholtz thought he achieved, was now a distant memory.

One of the leaders of the miners stated, "When we dispersed at the insistence of Keeney and Mooney, no further trouble would have taken place had not the constabulary, reinforced by mine guards, then attacked the Boone County Coal corporation mine near Sharples, which is a union stronghold in Logan county."[48] This time, the reassembled Redneck Army resumed their march, ignoring President Harding's proclamation for both sides to stand down by September 1, 1921. In the process, the miners took over roadways and points of passage, hijacked trains, and refused to turn aside without the clear intervention of federal troops. Knowing a direct assault on the mountain would be disastrous, the miners attempted to flank Chafin's defenders. Sheriff Chafin also seized this opportunity to up the ante, deploying his rented bi-planes to drop tear gas and pipe bombs loaded with TNT, targeting the invaders from the air.[49] "A message from Sheriff Chafin's headquarters read: Give my regards to the boys and kill all the red necks you can."[50] Upon seeing there was no hope to resolve this conflict with simple diplomacy, Bandholtz had seen enough and knew he must direct troops to the region.

Under orders from General Bandholtz, Captain John J. Wilson and his men were the first to make contact with Bill Blizzard. Wilson asked if Blizzard was the man in charge. "'I guess the boys'll listen to me all right.' Captain Wilson searched Blizzard and discovered he was carrying a pistol. The army officer asked him if he had a permit. Blizzard produced one signed by the sheriff of Kanawha County. Captain Wilson returned the gun."[51] Upon learning that the Captain would let only those miners with permits keep their guns, Blizzard slipped off to address the miners. When Blizzard's ragtag army came drifting out of the woods and hills to surrender, most of them

48. *Santa Ana Register*, Santa Ana, California, September 1, 1921.
49. *Athens Messenger*, Athens, Ohio, September 2, 1921.
50. Gerald Lively, *Daily Kos*, "Exploitation, Duplicity, Corruption, and Domestic Warfare…"
51. Blizzard, "When Miners March," p. 321.

presented themselves to the troops, empty-handed, their guns still left hidden deep in the woods and abandoned mines to be reclaimed later, if necessary.

The miners and their leadership believed the intervention of federal troops would aid their cause and bring national attention to their plight. The coal owners saw the military's arrival as a chance to finally destroy the UMWA, stop their union organizing, and deplete their financial coffers through endless litigation. The miners and their leadership were mistaken. The bitter conflict waged in the southern West Virginia coalfields did merit a brief but meaningless investigation from Washington. "The congressional committee, known as the Kenyon Committee, condemned the practice in Logan County of paying the sheriff and his deputies from funds contributed by the coal operators instead of exclusively from the public treasury, but no federal action resulted from the committee's work."[52] Things only got worse as the conflicts moved out of the battlefield and into the courtroom. After the miners laid down—or rather, hid—their weapons and returned to their homes, with many of them still living in tents, all three of their union leaders faced a court trial and the possibility of a hangman's rope.

"On the day after Christmas the three men [Frank Keeney, Fred Mooney, and Bill Blizzard] boarded a train for Logan and headed toward the county where no Union man had set foot without danger of mutilation or death," wrote William C. Blizzard, in *When Miners March*. "What treatment they would be accorded by Don Chafin they could not know, but they were aware of what was possible and it was not a pleasant prospect."[53] Despite his hatred for this trio of District 17 officials, even Sheriff Chafin and his deputies dared not give them the typical reception he generally delivered to union organizers who dared to breach his county line. "We shall not attempt to assess the role of Keeney, Blizzard and Mooney as regards their attitude and action in the 1921 march. All were later tried on murder charges and acquitted of same. Blizzard had the additional honor of being tried for treason against the State of West Virginia at the scene of the John Brown trials in Charles Town, West Virginia. He was acquitted..."[54]

---

52. Lively, *Daily Kos*, "Exploitation, Duplicity, Corruption, and Domestic Warfare..."
53. Blizzard, "When Miners March," p. 326.
54. Ibid, p. 276. Despite the fact an American citizen cannot be found guilty of committing treason against a state government, Bill Blizzard, Frank Keeney, and Fred Mooney, were indicted for those very crimes. The charge of treason

In his book, *Thunder in the Mountains*, Lon Savage wrote: "In October 1922, the executive committee of the United Mine Workers finally called off the strike. It had cost two million dollars, enough to bankrupt District 17 of the UMWA...Partly because of the failed strike in Mingo County, membership in the United Mine Workers in West Virginia slumped from its peak of about fifty thousand in 1920 to about six hundred in 1929. It was not until the Roosevelt administration that the mines of southern West Virginia were unionized. Once started, however, organization swiftly spread through the mines of the state in the 1930s."[55]

So ended the Battle of Blair Mountain, the most significant labor uprising in American history and the largest armed insurrection since the Civil War. One can indeed speculate that it was a war started by just one man, Charles E. Lively. Although Lively's whereabouts during the midst of the fighting are still uncertain, his name and actions were certainly on the lips and minds of every miner engaged in this bitter and bloody conflict. In addition, the record makes it clear that Charles E. Lively wasn't just a minor or ancillary figure in the coal mine wars; he may indeed be the primary figure. In the hearts and minds of those striking West Virginia miners, the spark had already been kindled. Lively's actions only served to throw gasoline upon them. Moreover, when the UMWA later erected a monument upon the grave of Sid Hatfield, the stone stated: "His murder triggered the miners' rebellion at the Battle of Blair Mountain."[56]

"While one need not look far to find accounts describing the troops as suppressing the revolt or defeated miners surrendering, the reality at the time was likely quite different," penned Wess Harris, in the book, *Written in Blood*. "Archeologist Harvard Ayers, a longtime Blair Mountain researcher, is clear: 'Absent the feds, I believe the miners may have overrun the coal operators, and it would have been a bloody mess.' When troops arrived, miners did not envision defeat. Far from surrendering, miners welcomed the troops as would any weary front-line fighter being offered a chance to withdraw from the front and be replaced by fresh troops. Our Boys had arrived. Robert Shogan reminds us that as the miners marched from Blair Mountain, 'many of them waved American flags.' It is noteworthy that Blizzard, known

---

can only be applied to acts committed against the federal government; however, for citizens of West Virginia during the coal mine wars, the Constitution was little more than a beloved concept.
55. Savage, "Thunder in the Mountains," p. 166.
56. Ibid, p. 167.

but unnamed leader of the miners, was not arrested as would be any leader of a rebellion. He was free to go and allowed to keep his weapon," Harris continued. "Hardly how a defeated rebel is treated! Blair Mountain was one battle that the people won... Historians of all political leanings have all too often been complicit in repeating tales of defeat. Looking back, Blair Mountain was a victory by people no longer willing to be controlled, exploited, and violently abused from above,"[57]

Other than Charles E. Lively, none of those directly involved in the assassination of Hatfield and Chambers had long to live upon this earth. None of them lived to see the age of fifty. A new decade had scarcely dawned before these three, loyal and trusted Baldwin-Felts agents, men who lived by the sword, Bill Salter, Hughey Lucas, and Buster Pence, were all dead, victims of unexpected and, in some cases, extremely violent circumstances.

Bill Salter, while working as a McDowell County deputy sheriff was in War, West Virginia, where a Sunday baseball game was taking place in September of 1923. Will Jackson and Jim Holley soon became involved in a bitter dispute, after Holley lost a bet on the game. "It is said Jim Holley, colored, a companion of Jackson, had laid a bet with a white man, name unknown, and the white man had won. A disagreement followed the game and Holley is said to have bitten the white man on the cheek, and in return had been hit on the head with a rock. Jackson is said to have fired at the white man, the bullet grazing the man's head and knocking him down. Jackson started to run." Upon seeing the altercation, Salter "commandeered a horse and started in pursuit" of the suspect, Will Jackson, who was likely the same individual who shot and wounded Buster Pence in 1915.[58]

At some point during the escape attempt, which lasted for nearly a mile, Salter apparently shot Will Jackson in the back. "It is said Jackson got behind a big tree and ambushed Salter. Salter was shot through the chest, near the heart, the bullet coming out the left shoulder."[59] Hit by the slug from Jackson's gun, the deputy was knocked from the saddle and fell to the ground. Upon seeing the condition of his pursuer, Jackson, still armed, approached the wounded and helpless officer. "As Salter looked up at him, the alleged murderer is said to have fired a second

57. Harris, "Written in Blood," p. 98.
58. *Bluefield Daily Telegraph*, Bluefield, West Virginia, September 4, 1923.;
    Bluefield Daily Telegraph, Bluefield, West Virginia, May 2, 1915.
59. *Bluefield Daily Telegraph*, Bluefield, West Virginia, September 4, 1923.

shot, the bullet going out the base of the skull, just behind the left ear. The bullet was found in Salter's coat collar, and is said to have been a .38 calibre. The shooting of William Salter is said to have been cold-blooded. The first shot was fired at a distance of less than two feet, while the second shot was from a pistol held close to Salter's head."[60] Bill Salter, "regarded as one of the best officers in the county," was only 43-years old at the time of his death and left behind his wife, Thursa Salter.[61]

At a time when the nation's front-page headlines were dominated by the kidnapping of Charles Lindbergh's baby, Hughey Lucas, a Mercer County deputy sheriff and prohibition officer, became embroiled in a dispute which quickly turned deadly. On the first weekend of March, 1932, after a night of drinking during America's Prohibition era, it was alleged that an intoxicated Lucas pulled a gun on Charles Dillon and demanded that he drive Lucas home. The details are sketchy because the reports and testimony vary; however, while switching automobiles in a store parking lot around four o'clock in the morning, Dillon claimed that Lucas slapped his wife or said something inappropriate to the woman.[62] Dillon warned the deputy to stop his behavior. When Lucas, "a reputed womanizer," repeated his earlier actions, Dillon shot him, inflicting "a bullet wound at the base of the brain."[63] Hughey Lucas, 48, died the next day and was survived by his wife, Janette, and children. Dillon was acquitted of the incident, but sentenced to serve six months for illegally carrying a pistol. Approximately a month later, Dillon was granted parole.[64]

The end for George Washington "Buster" Pence, although it didn't occur through the same violent means that took both Salter and Lucas, was most certainly unexpected, befalling him just before Christmas in 1929. "Death occurred suddenly yesterday to Buster Pence, 46, at his home, 309 Rogers Street. Although he had been in failing health for the past year, his condition had not been considered serious and his passing came as a distinct shock to relatives."[65] The long-time, Baldwin-Felts agent was survived by his wife, Amy Pence.

60. Ibid.
61. Ibid.
62. *Bluefield Daily Telegraph*, Bluefield, West Virginia, April 27, 1932.
63. Find A Grave, https://www.findagrave.com/memorial/17660463/hugh-henry-lucas, Hugh Henry Lucas, November 20, 2019.; Bluefield Daily Telegraph, Bluefield, West Virginia, March 6, 1932.
64. *Bluefield Daily Telegraph*, Bluefield, West Virginia, May 8, 1932.
65. *Bluefield Daily Telegraph*, Bluefield, West Virginia, December 19, 1929.

For Charles E. Lively, unlike his fellow agents from the McDowell County courthouse lawn, his death did not occur in scarcely a mere decade. In fact, the most dangerous man in the West Virginia-Colorado coal mine wars survived through several more decades. Although Number Nine's usefulness to Baldwin-Felts had reached its logical conclusion before the end of 1922, Lively's love and loyalty to the agency, along with its leadership, remained firm for many years. This claim is substantiated by the pictures Lively prominently displayed on the mantel of his residence.[66] Although the detective's relationship with Baldwin-Felts had been severed, Charles E. Lively's long and disturbing trail of personal transgressions were far from finished.

66. *Beckley Post Herald*, Beckley, West Virginia, June 6, 1937.

Chapter 11

Picking Up the Pieces

After the shooting on the courthouse steps, the acquittal in Chambers' murder, and his subsequent release from the Hatfield murder indictment, Lively seemed to disappear from public view for almost two full years, leaving it uncertain as to his actions and employment for that time. Charles E. Lively was seen again in October 1923, with the former Baldwin-Felts detective now working as a McDowell County Deputy Sheriff and Prohibition officer, a position Lively started sometime around January 1921.[1]

It is also interesting to note that despite being acquitted on capital murder charges for killing Hatfield and Chambers, Lively was still allowed to work for McDowell County Sheriff Bill Hatfield, the lawman who specifically guaranteed that no harm would come to Sid Hatfield when he appeared in Welch for trial. The fact that Lively remained one of his deputies also lends more credibility to the allegations that Sheriff Hatfield's pre-trial vacation to Virginia's Craig Healing Springs was likely paid for by Thomas Felts' and was part of his larger conspiracy to get revenge on Smiling Sid. Equally disturbing was Sheriff W.J. Hatfield's own statement regarding his absence from Welch on that fateful day, as if he could have done nothing to prevent the violence on the courthouse lawn. "I do not think it would have made any difference," he said.[2]

Not surprisingly, this latest public appearance of Lively also found him embroiled in controversy, ending with charges being brought against him and another appearance in court. Lively had gone to the home of Charles Daugherty, in Turkey Gap, West Virginia, with a warrant to arrest Daugherty's son, Paul, for stealing an automobile. The accounts of the story are conflicted, but Lively's version was that the father lied to him, allowing the son a chance to flee the home by jumping out the window. "Lively then arrested Daugherty on the charge of assisting his son to escape."[3] Lively also claimed the father resisted arrest. But

1. *Bluefield Daily Telegraph*, Bluefield, Virginia, January 25, 1921.
2. Savage, "Thunder in the Mountains," p. 74.
3. *Bluefield Daily Telegraph*, Bluefield, Virginia, October 20, 1923.

on one item, both Lively and Daugherty were in total agreement: "Lively drew his gun, which he used with telling affect on the head of Daugherty, inflicting an ugly wound just below the ear and rendering him unconscious."[4] After striking Daugherty on the head with his pistol, Lively was charged with felonious assault and held on a five-hundred dollar bond. The trial was held several months later, with Lively continuing to perform his duties while awaiting trial for the Daugherty incident.

In December 1923, L.R. Brown and Frank Brooks surrendered to Officer Lively and were jailed on murder charges. Three men, Brown, Brooks, and William Bowman had been hunting together when a heated argument ensued between two of them. Following their altercation, Brooks shot Bowman with a shotgun. Brown was released soon after L.R. Brooks confessed he was indeed at fault.[5]

Lively, while acting as a prohibition officer, also made arrests relating to liquor charges in December 1923. "Charged with having twenty-eight pints of moonshine in his possession, Frank Marsz, was arrested yesterday by Officer. C.E. Lively. He was fined $200 and costs and given two months on the county roads."[6] In the days and months to follow, it can be speculated that Lively, the prohibition officer, may have arrested those possessing illegal liquor, while at the same time being guilty of withholding some of the evidence for his own consumption later.

In what today is known as "unlawful force," a jury found Lively guilty of "unlawful wounding," on February 7, 1924, for striking Daugherty on the head with his pistol.[7] "The punishment for this offense is from one to ten years in the penitentiary. A motion to set aside the verdict was made by attorneys for the defendant, which will be heard at a later date."[8] From what is already known about the former Baldwin-Felts agent, there is every reason to suspect that Lively was indeed guilty of this crime, and pistol whipped the father in a fit of uncontrolled rage, behavior which would be strikingly consistent with Lively's later conduct, reflecting actions taken with members of the public and his own family. About two weeks later, also in February 1924, Lively was refused the granting of a

4. Ibid.
5. *Bluefield Daily Telegraph*, Bluefield, West Virginia, December 27, 1923.
6. Ibid.
7. *Welch Daily News*, Welch, West Virginia, February 5, 1924.
8. *Bluefield Daily Telegraph*, Bluefield, Virginia, February 9, 1924.

new trial for his felonious assault on Daugherty, but "was granted a stay of 45 days in which to apply to the Appellate court for a writ of error and supersedes."[9] He was made to put up a bond of one-thousand dollars. Lively was eventually fined one-hundred dollars and given sixty days for his crime.[10]

A man of harsh and intemperate mood swings, conditions which were no doubt compounded by his increased drinking, it is readily apparent that Charles E. Lively was something of a bully, the sort of man who should never have been granted the sacred trust of keeping the law. Along with that, it also appears that the former undercover operative obviously learned nothing from his conviction in the Daugherty assault. In July 1924, Lively was arrested at his home in Keystone, West Virginia, and jailed for allegedly beating up a grand jury witness against him. "The witness who Lively charged with bringing about the indictments is D. Farley, who lives at Bottom Creek. After the indictments were reported, Farley, who is a cripple as a result of the kick of a mule, said Lively came to his place and made threats he would kill him."[11] The news story pointed out that the officers who came to arrest him were expecting trouble, since it was known that Lively, with or without a pistol license, routinely carried a pair of guns, either for his own protection or the possible intimidation of others. When officers arrived to arrest him, the news reports said, "Lively was drunk and heavily armed. He did not resist however."[12]

Increasingly, it's apparent to researchers that Lively's life and career had entered a death spiral, almost from the moment his employment with Baldwin-Felts ended, culminating in numerous reports of illegal and excessive drinking and other acts of disorderly behavior. While serving with the Agency, his entire life had been grounded in being an undercover operative. So important was that job to him, Lively kept a scrapbook of his exploits, an item which—although rumored to have suffered some significant damage—is still in the hands of his descendants today.

Baldwin-Felts had been Lively's one source of strength and stability, giving him a reason to swear off the normal, everyday vices that might have otherwise detracted from his one all-

9. *Welch Daily News*, Welch, West Virginia, February 29, 1924.
10. Transcript for Charles E. Lively, Federal Bureau of Investigation, Washington, D.C., October 29, 1937.
11. *Bluefield Daily Telegraph*, Bluefield, Virginia, July 19, 1924.
12. Ibid.

encompassing desire to be the best agent possible. But with that status removed, it appears that Lively no longer had the necessary incentive to present any semblance of being a law-abiding citizen. In addition, with his no longer being under the protective auspices of Baldwin-Felts, Lively no longer had anybody around to bail him out of the trouble he increasingly found himself facing. And as his future life indicated, those problems also carried into his marriage and homelife.

In August 1924, after being indicted for driving an automobile while intoxicated, Lively was found not guilty by a jury. One of the key witnesses, Mrs. Morrison [First name unreported], failed to appear for the hearing. There is no evidence that Lively made any threats to the woman, as he had done to a witness in an earlier grand jury hearing. The allegations involved a dispute at a filling station in Kimball, West Virginia. While gassing up their automobiles, Lively allegedly came over to the other occupant's vehicle and said something offensive to Mrs. Morrison and tried to force the woman to leave the automobile. As a result, a dispute occurred with the other occupants in Mrs. Morrison's vehicle. "Lively testified on the stand that he had had no liquor and Mrs. Lively also denied on the stand that he had been drinking."[13]

In October 1924, it was reported: "Among the cases of this term are several against C.E. Lively who has been indicted by the last grand jury on several more charges of carrying pistols and possessing liquor in addition to one of having intimidated a witness, D. Farley, who gave testimony against him before the Grand Jury."[14] Scarcely a few months later, Lively ran afoul of the law again, once more caught with bootleg liquor and carrying guns without a license. In February 1925, while awaiting sentence in McDowell County, Lively was living in Logan County and posing as an officer. "When arrested, it was said, Lively had two pistols on his person and a quantity of moonshine."[15]

"Dry agents raided his room at the Y.M.C.A. hotel where he had registered a few days earlier as 'C.E. Lester.' Commissioner Hager issued a search warrant on which the room was entered and the agents declared they found a pint of moonshine whiskey there."[16] Marshal Reynolds recognized the former Baldwin-Felts

13. *Bluefield Daily Telegraph*, Bluefield, Virginia, August 3, 1924.
14. *Bluefield Daily Telegraph*, Bluefield, Virginia, October 12, 1924.
15. *Bluefield Daily Telegraph*, Bluefield, Virginia, February 6, 1925.
16. *Charleston Daily Mail*, Charleston, West Virginia, February 9, 1925.

agent and began questioning him and "upon asking him a few questions learned he wanted to act bad in Logan County, but his chance to pull off any bad stuff was brief, as he was arrested as soon as the officer searched him."[17] When Lively failed to present the ten-thousand dollar bond, pending his indictment, he was removed from incarceration in Logan County and transferred to the city jail in Huntington, West Virginia.

During this period, it appears that Lively's home life may have also been slowly deteriorating in much the same way as his professional career. Charles and his wife, Icie, continued to bear children throughout this period, but the seeds of discontent had already started to germinate and take root. Although he was no longer working for Baldwin-Felts, the habits of his past were hard to break. Lively was often gone at night, getting drunk, and sleeping at the YMCA, and generally on the wrong side of the law. There is also overwhelming evidence that Lively was unfaithful to his wife. The very fabric of his life for this once proud detective was beginning to unravel. Along with the tatters in his home life, there is also no clear-cut explanation as to how Lively escaped serving many years in prison for the multiple criminal charges he faced. It can be speculated that Lively's service, via his years with Baldwin-Felts, afforded him some substantial collateral with the coal companies, favors he may have cashed in to escape the mounting charges with local officials. But the charges against Lively had only started.

In September 1929, Lively faced the most serious allegations of his life, other than the charges related to the killing of Hatfield and Chambers. The former detective was working as a mine guard in Fairmont, West Virginia, employed by Fairmont-Chicago Coal Company, at its Chesapeake mine. Lively was "formally charged with criminal assault on the person of a thirteen-year-old daughter of a miner at Chesapeake. The little girl charges she was assaulted several months ago at Chesapeake."[18] The other man indicted in the case was a Chesapeake miner named Carroll, but it was unclear whether the man's first name was either Joe or William, names which varied according to the newspaper account one might read.

"Carroll and Lively were indicted jointly. The girl declared that she often attended moving picture shows here with Carroll and that he assaulted her on more than one occasion as they

17. *Bluefield Daily Telegraph*, Bluefield, Virginia, February 6, 1925.
18. *Bluefield Daily Telegraph*, Bluefield, Virginia, October 3, 1925.

returned home."[19] William Carroll later confessed to the charge and was sentenced to "life imprisonment in the state penitentiary at Moundsville."[20] Lively, on the other hand, was acquitted in the case after the jury deliberated for only a couple hours. The newspaper reported: "The little girl is still held by the authorities and will be committed to a home for girls," undoubtedly language of the time which indicated the girl had likely become pregnant as a result of William Carroll's rape.[21]

One can only wonder how Lively became embroiled in this case. There can be no question that the girl was there when it happened; she certainly knew if either Carroll or Lively had truly assaulted her. But why was the jury so quick to find Lively not guilty? Was Lively the victim of a false accusation, based on the hatred reserved for him in coal mining communities around the state? Perhaps the girl's father, after learning his daughter could be pregnant, looked to punish the man who harmed his daughter, and simply threw in Lively's name to gain a little payback for his brother miners. It could also be speculated that Lively was indeed guilty of the crime, but his years of loyal service to the coal companies were substantially rewarded with a favorable verdict. Perhaps the truth will never be known in this case. It is simply one more of the ever-mounting questions regarding the detective's life, career, and reputation.

But Lively's troubles regarding the incident were far from over. Upon learning of the rape allegations, along with Lively's employment at the Chesapeake mine, Van A. Bittner, chief international representative of the United Mine Workers in northern West Virginia "sent a telegram to Governor Gore at Charleston, protesting the presence in this field of C.E. Lively. He also said the governor had told him 'Lively could not work as a mine guard for any coal company in northern West Virginia.'"[22] Bittner also "requested the governor to have Lively sent out of the community."[23]

Once again, another five years passed before much more was known regarding how Charles E. Lively fared. The 1930 federal census lists Lively, then with nine children, as returning to the coal mines.[24] In what capacity Lively was working, as a mine

19. *Charleston Daily Mail*, Charleston, Virginia, October 13, 1925.
20. Ibid.
21. *Bluefield Daily Telegraph*, Bluefield, West Virginia, October 14, 1925.
22. *Bluefield Daily Telegraph*, Bluefield, West Virginia, September 29, 1925.
23. Ibid.
24. 1930 Federal Census, Raleigh County, West Virginia, Shady Springs District, Ancestry, www.Ancestry.com.

guard or a miner, there is no indication. It is known, however, that Lively was not opposed to employing aliases; therefore, it is not unreasonable to assume the former undercover operative may have returned to his roots and sought gainful employment in the mines, under an assumed name. Moreover, since photographs of Lively are indeed rare, and Social Security was not yet in existence, a number which made it easier to track individuals from place-to-place, it is entirely possible that Lively could find employment in many of the coal mines throughout the state and escape detection, just so long as his real name wasn't discovered. In addition, the UMWA was little more than a broken and powerless organization after the Battle of Blair Mountain and its subsequent trials, and the union's former influence wouldn't again be realized until sometime during the presidential administration of Franklin Roosevelt. This also made it easier for anti-union individuals such as Charles E. Lively to find work in the state's coalfields.

As further proof that Lively was indeed a man with many lives, the detective bounced back from the Chesapeake rape allegations, reclaimed some personal semblance of normalcy, and found another job in law enforcement. In February 1931, it's reported that Deputy Sheriff Charles Lively arrested Dora Miller for shooting her husband, Charles F. Miller, in Glen White, West Virginia. Her husband was reported to be "in a precarious condition in the Beckley hospital." Dora Miller claimed "that she fired in self-defense." There were no witnesses to the shooting. Deputy Lively took Mrs. Miller to the Raleigh County jail for incarceration.[25]

Lively's work in law enforcement continued into March 1933, when the following story was reported: "Special Officer Charles Lively arrested a man giving the name of James Hill, of Charleston, last night, and booked him on a misdemeanor count. Lively said that Hill indulged in several games of pool in the recreation hall at Glen White and then refused to settle the score."[26] This arrest of Jim Hill also coincided with the birth of Lively's tenth and last child, Paul Lively, who was born to them the same month.

To all those around them, things might have appeared to be good between Charles E. Lively and his wife, Icie, while they made their home in the town of Mount Hope, West Virginia.[27]

25. *Charleston Daily Mail*, Charleston, West Virginia, February 2, 1931.
26. *Beckley Post Herald*, Beckley, West Virginia, March 31, 1933.
27. *Beckley Post Herald*, Beckley, West Virginia, June 26, 1937.

In the life of the former undercover operative, however, things were often not the way they appeared. A little more than four years later, the troubles Lively faced in his turbulent homelife came to a bitter and violent breaking point.

Although his latest employment certainly wasn't a job with Baldwin-Felts, one that Lively truly loved, he was at least an officer of the law, obviously the next best thing for a man who spent that many years as a detective. In June 1931, the Beckley Post Herald reported: "Mike Misky drew a fine of $10 and costs on a charge of being drunk in public. The arrest was credited to Deputy Sheriff Charles Lively."[28]

As Lively's relationships at home were crumbling, the former agent soldiered on as if nothing was wrong. Maybe Lively didn't see it, perhaps he didn't care. Lively kept working in law enforcement; he maintained appearances, behavior which the detective repeatedly conducted for years as an undercover operative for Baldwin-Felts. But changes were coming his way, life altering transformations in both Lively's homelife and for the nation as a whole. Only a matter of mere months before the Volstead Act and Prohibition were repealed, Lively was noted making an illegal liquor arrest in West Virginia.

In May 1933, Lively discovered a moonshine still, "ingeniously hidden in a 'dug-out' on the outskirts of Sophia, [West Virginia]."[29] He arrested two people, James Polk and Tina Pittman, who also faced federal charges in the case. The newspaper stated: "Special Officer Charles Lively is credited with discovering the plant. His suspicion was excited when he observed smoke billowing from the earth near the Polk farm, and subsequent investigation by the officer revealed the 'dug-out' in which the still was secreted."[30]

The record indicates that, as an agent, investigator, and a lawman, Charles E. Lively generally excelled at discovering those things which were often hidden. In his dual responsibilities as a husband and father, however, Lively failed to see the errors and shortcomings in his own life, and make the necessary changes to correct them. Those personal character flaws eventually led to him committing other acts of great violence.

---

28. *Beckley Post Herald*, Beckley, West Virginia, June 30, 1931.
29. *Beckley Post Herald*, Beckley, West Virginia, May 5, 1933.
30. Ibid.

Chapter 12

The Battles of Mount Hope

There can be no question that the repeated months of leaving his wife behind while working undercover for Baldwin-Felts must have taken a huge toll on Charles E. Lively's marriage. From the record, it is clear that Lively made brief returns to his home, perhaps either during or just after his assignments. It also appears that on those occasional homecomings, he and Icie often conceived another child, only to have the detective leave soon after on another mission for his beloved Agency. It is known that Lively strayed from his marriage vows; therefore, it is quite likely that his wife may have known or suspected his unfaithfulness. Perhaps his wife also sensed that all was not well with Lively, in much the same way that Fred Mooney suspected something was amiss with him when Mooney refused to spend the night at Lively's house seventeen years earlier.

In Williamson and at Washington D.C., Lively testified he gave no regards to the oath he took as a union man; therefore, it isn't unreasonable to assume he exhibited the same level of commitment to the vows he took at the alter or when sitting upon the witness stand. It is clear that Lively was excellent at his chosen profession, but it also seems he was equally bad in fulfilling his crucial roles as husband and father. Such a condition is not unusual in an individual who routinely gives everything to his work. Moreover, it can be shown that Lively's constant absence in his home may have also been a contributing factor to the criminal activities committed by a couple of his sons.

Lively and his family were still living in the West Virginia community of Mount Hope, in June 1937. By the mid-1930s, the relationship between Charles E. Lively and his wife had deteriorated, perhaps beyond repair. The lucrative, second job Lively once enjoyed with Baldwin-Felts was gone forever, no doubt adding to his dissatisfaction with life. For someone who had once been a trusted and loyal agent, he often seemed to fail miserably at the things in his personal life. Lively's employment as a special officer had obviously come to an end, because he was working as a mining foreman "in the Siltix mine. Recently, according to his family, he had told office attaches at the mine script (sic) office not to allow them any groceries at the store."[1]

There was clearly no peace and harmony dwelling in the Lively household, a location where Lively apparently placed no value on his duties as husband and father, and the pictures on his mantel reminded all who entered there of his past glories as a Baldwin-Felts detective. In order to make ends meet during the years following the Great Depression, and especially because of Lively's recent refusal to provide for his family, it was probably his wife who decided she needed to earn some money by having other individuals, non-family members, boarding inside the Lively home. "On the walls at his home, a log structure of (sic) the center of town, covered with weatherboarding, pictures of Baldwin and Felts are posted above the mantelpiece, and a son related that Lively had frequently told of his work while with this bureau."[2] That was the home of Charles E. Lively in 1937, a tinderbox waiting for a spark.

On Friday, June 25, Lively's youngest son, Paul, who was only four-years-old at the time, took a minor tumble in their home. According to Lively's wife, Paul "fell over overalls he was carrying."[3] After stumbling, the child started to cry and blamed his brother Russell, 12, for tripping him. Upon hearing the commotion, an enraged, Lively came storming into the room, looking to punish Russell, who he saw as the offending child. Russell appealed to his father and claimed he did nothing to his younger brother. He maintained the child just fell, but Russell's explanation apparently fell on deaf ears.

When the incident occurred, Lively's wife, Icie, described her husband as "a funny man who takes funny spells."[4] Along with that statement, Icie added that "her husband had been 'pouting around' for several days."[5] His son, Charles Albert, once wrote this about Lively. "I know up until I was 12, I was terrified of my father. He had a split personality and was a different person from one day to the next."[6] These various, albeit similar characterizations of Charles E. Lively can certainly lead one to believe that the former agent suffered from some form of mental or chemical imbalance, perhaps a condition which would be labeled as being

1. *Beckley Raleigh Register*, Beckley, West Virginia, June 28, 1937.
2. *Beckley Post Herald*, Beckley, West Virginia, June 26, 1937.
3. *Beckley Raleigh Register*, Beckley, West Virginia, June 28, 1937.
4. *Beckley Post Herald*, Beckley, West Virginia, June 26, 1937.
5. *Beckley Raleigh Register*, Beckley, West Virginia, June 28, 1937.
6. Blizzard, William C, and Harris, Wess, ed., "When Miners March," A letter from Charles A. Lively to William C. Blizzard.

'bipolar' today, and could now be treated and controlled with pharmaceutical drugs.

After the child's accident, Charles E. Lively was obviously unsatisfied with his son's explanation of the incident and was looking for someone to punish. Lively's son, Arnold, insisted that Russell had done nothing to harm the child. Apparently, Gordon Lively, 16, must have also exchanged some bitter words with his father, especially in the wake of their previous altercations. Members of the family said "that Gordon and his father quarreled after the youth 'took up' for a younger brother."[7] It is also clear that Gordon's intervention in behalf of his younger brother didn't set well with his father, who ordered him to take the punishment in Russell's stead, to which Gordon replied, "In a minute, when I get a drink,' and then went into the kitchen."[8] That is when the rancor between Lively and his son, Gordon, escalated to the point of violence.

The difficulties between Lively and his son, Gordon, were obviously long-standing. "Everett Lively, 24, of Stotesbury, said his father several years ago 'locked Gordon up' in the vegetable cellar, and that the boy only escaped by using a hacksaw to cut bars across one window of the cellar. 'We had some trouble about that,' Everett said of his father today, 'but outside of that he always treated me right.'"[9]

After Charles E. Lively's argument with his son, the former detective was fuming when he left the room. "Meanwhile Lively himself, according to a roomer in the home, had gone to a front room; when Gordon went into the kitchen the father passed through a hallway, across a side porch into the yard, and approached the kitchen from the rear of the house. He fired two shots through a screen door at Gordon, according to the members of the family."[10] Gordon dropped his cup and crumpled to the floor, seriously wounded from the first shot, which hit him in the neck, the second slug failing to strike its mark on the already falling young man. "'I saw him come out of the front room a moment before the shooting,' said Kinder [a boarder in the Lively home], who loads coal at Cranberry, 'and after the shooting I helped bring the boy in here (into his own room) and put him on the bed."[11]

---

7. *Beckley Post Herald*, Beckley, West Virginia, June 26, 1937.
8. *Beckley Raleigh Register*, Beckley, West Virginia, June 28, 1937.
9. *Beckley Post Herald*, Beckley, West Virginia, June 29, 1937.
10. *Beckley Raleigh Register*, Beckley, West Virginia, June 28, 1937.
11. Ibid.

After the shooting, Lively went to a nearby neighbor's house, told them he just shot his son, and asked them to call the police. After that, Lively remained in the yard, gun in hand, waiting for the police to arrive. Gordon was transported to the hospital in Montgomery. Lively was placed under arrest and taken to the jail in Fayetteville, until the extent of Gordon's injuries was fully known.

It is doubtful anyone will ever know for sure whether or not Lively meant to kill his son or just to scare him. Perhaps Lively only meant to intimidate or threaten the boy, the bullet possibly striking Gordon by accident. It is known, however, that Lively was excellent with a gun, thereby making this theory unreliable. According to retired Peace Officer, Sheriff Jim Wilson, who served in both Denton and Crockett counties in Texas and is a handgun defense trainer and shooting authority, it is unlikely that the screen door may have altered the trajectory of Lively's shot. "About any of them back then were going to be a round-nose, lead bullet. I don't believe it would deflect it very much. It might deflect it," he said, "microscopically. More than likely, it would have just punched right on through that screen. It would be pretty much dead on." With that information in mind, one is left with only the likelihood that Lively, in a fit of anger, actually meant to shoot Gordon and possibly kill him. "I could see circumstances where people would do that," Sheriff Wilson added, "if he had a temper, and something was on him at the moment, and especially if he had a drink or two. As an officer I wouldn't be surprised if something like that happened. Families fight, you know."

The record definitely indicates that this family did indeed fight. "Lillian Lively told of violent family quarrels in the days preceding the shooting. 'Last night, he (her father) doubled a telephone wire and beat Mother,' the girl said."[12] Besides the woman's noticeable bruises and lacerations, Mrs. Icie Lively confirmed her daughter's account of the previous night's incident, when she explained that her husband swung the telephone wire at Russell, but struck her instead. "I wouldn't say he meant to strike me, but he did hit me."[13] The daughter, Lillian, went on to say that when the police arrived, they were just returning home, because "she and her mother hitch-hiked to Fayetteville to get aid from the law in forcing him to provide for the family."[14] In fact, one of the sons, Charles Albert Lively, had

12. *Beckley Post Herald*, Beckley, West Virginia, June 26, 1937.
13. *Beckley Raleigh Register*, Beckley, West Virginia, June 28, 1937.
14. *Beckley Sunday Register*, Beckley, West Virginia, June 27, 1937.

already personally assumed the financial responsibility for meeting his mother's household needs.[15] After the shooting of her son, Mrs. Lively believed that her husband would try to explain away his actions by alleging self-defense. "He's going to claim the boys threw fruit jars at him, but that isn't true. They told me that Arnold started throwing fruit jars at him after the shooting, but they hadn't thrown any before that."[16]

To the man's credit, and also lending some credibility to the speculation that he actually meant to harm his son and retrospectively regretted the deed, Lively refused to offer any explanations, justifications, or details for his actions in the shooting. The prosecutor, Carl Vickers, who charged Lively with malicious wounding, said Lively readily acknowledged the shooting to him. "'I've been advised not to talk,' the former Baldwin-Felts detective said. 'You can see my lawyer, and if he wants to say anything, that's all right with me.'"[17] Charles E. Lively later waived his hearing and was held without bond, waiting for the grand jury to issue an indictment.

After the shooting, the officials at a Montgomery hospital believed that Gordon would fully recover from the gunshot wound to his neck, which just missed potentially damaging his spinal cord. "Members of the family said that they had talked with the injured son, and that he seemed in good humor, Friday, before passing into a coma, he told a brother that he was going to 'get even' with his father, and added 'he's my meat now.'"[18] Those statements by Gordon proved to be harbingers of future violence within the Lively household. Later, with Gordon "out of danger,"[19] Lively's wife and the children still living at home fully cooperated with the authorities in the investigation of the incident. Gordon soon returned home, with no lingering traces of paralysis from his injury. In July 1937, Lively was indicted for the crime of shooting his son, "with intent to maim, disfigure, disable and kill."[20] Later that year, October 1937, family members willingly gave testimony in the trial. Charles E. Lively pleaded, "Not guilty of malicious wounding."[21]

15. Ibid.
16. *Beckley Raleigh Register*, Beckley, West Virginia, June 28, 1937.
17. Ibid.
18. *Beckley Sunday Register*, Beckley, West Virginia, June 27, 1937.
19. *Beckley Post Herald*, Beckley, West Virginia, July 1, 1937.
20. Circuit Court Indictment, State of West Virginia, Fayette County.
21. State of West Virginia vs. Felony Indictment #221 Charles E. Lively, Fayette County Circuit Court, Mrs. L.S. Tully, Clerk.

Despite Lively's plea, the court ruled: "It is, therefore, adjudged and ordered that the said Charles E. Lively be confined in the penitentiary of this State on the aforesaid plea for a period of eighteen months, pay the costs of this proceeding, and that he be further dealt with according to law. And the guard duly authorized and sent by the Warden of the penitentiary shall as soon as may be after adjournment of this court safely remove from the jail of this county and convey to the penitentiary of this State at Moundsville the said Charles E. Lively, where he shall be kept in confinement at hard labor for and during the period of eighteen months, and the prisoner is remanded to jail to await the execution of sentence."[22]

On November 5, 1938, released before the full execution of his term (having served only a year) Charles E. Lively was freed from the prison at Moundsville, West Virginia. Approximately three weeks after his release, Lively returned to his home in Mount Hope. Obviously unwelcome to reside there any longer, the former detective simply returned to collect his things from the Lively home. It was at that time, Lively was once again involved in another act of violence, this time at the hands of his son.

"Police said the father, C.E. Lively, accompanied by Chief of Police Jess Spade came to the home this morning and gathered his belongings from the house to take to Stotesbury where the father got a job. Spade and the elder Lively, police continued, packed his clothes into a trunk. Then Lively went to the bus station to buy a ticket, caught a bus, and asked the driver to stop at the home for the large trunk, still sitting on the lawn. The driver, F.E. Holdren said: 'I was standing with my shoulder rubbing Lively's. I heard a noise, and asked Lively if the trunk had blown up. He groaned and answered 'No. That damn boy just shot me.'"[23] Although he may have been struck by the shotgun's wadding or touched by some of the buckshot, Holdren was uninjured from the incident and phoned the law. Lively was treated and released, the doctors initially fearing that he would lose the use of his arm. Gordon was arrested and taken to jail. His father, the former Baldwin-Felts agent, offered no cooperation to authorities in their efforts to prosecute his son. His only comment to authorities after being hit by a load of buckshot was, "I'm ruined."[24]

22. Ibid.
23. *Beckley Sunday Register*, Beckley, West Virginia, November 6, 1938.
24. Ibid.

Following the shooting, and speaking to reporters from his jail cell, Gordon said that he "stole the gun from a roomer and shot him."[25] He later went on to explain: "'I guess I was just crazy,' he said with a half-smile. 'I couldn't stand the sight of the old man. He had told one of our roomers that he would kill me and Arnold (in the state penitentiary serving a term for breaking and entering) as soon as he got a chance. I shot low so I wouldn't hit anyone else,' Gordon said. 'When he was in the house with Spade he whispered to mother that he wished the house would go up in flames and her with it. That made me mad. When he shot me last year, it was because I tried to stop him from beating her and my little brother with a telephone wire.'"[26] The entire interview was punctuated with Gordon Lively constantly "rising from his cell-bed and hanging by the bars."[27] He was also photographed there, smiling and seemingly in good spirits.

On November 5, 1938, the same day that Charles E. Lively had been shot by his son and Gordon had been incarcerated for the attempt on his father's life—on that same day—the family also learned this fearful news: "Word was received here that Everett Lively of Stotesbury is in critical condition following a mine accident in which the bit in a coal cutting machine struck both his legs. Members of the family said they fear for the older brother's life—and that he has been calling for his father, who is in the McKendree hospital receiving treatment for an injured shoulder, which is filled with gun shot."[28] Although it is unknown what he wanted with his father, it is speculated that Everett Lively wanted to persuade Charles E. Lively to once again begin providing for the needs of his mother and siblings, a responsibility Everett had taken on before his father shot Gordon and was sentenced to prison. It is unclear whether Charles E. Lively ever consented to meet with his wounded son, Everett, who was later reported to be on the mend, "very slowly."[29] It also appears that Everett Lively's remarkable recovery also displayed signs of the same dogged resilience often seen in his detective father, who was injured in the Colorado coal mine fall in 1910.

When Charles E. Lively shot his son Gordon, the family rallied around each other to testify against their father. However, when Gordon later used a shotgun to wound his father, the

25. *Charleston Gazette*, Charleston, West Virginia, November 6, 1938.
26. *Beckley Sunday Register*, Beckley, West Virginia, November 6, 1938.
27. Ibid.
28. *Beckley Raleigh Register*, Beckley, West Virginia, November 7, 1938.
29. Ibid.

family united behind Gordon and were only concerned with somehow keeping him out of prison. Russell, the thirteen-year-old child, who had initially been the one Lively tried to beat with a phone cord when Gordon came to his aid, a situation which gave rise to this bitter family feud, even presented a passionate appeal to keep his brother at home. "I sure hope we can help Gordon. Gordon has always been good to me and mother, and we think the world of him. We don't want him to go to jail—he was too good to us. He helped earn a living after the old man was sent to jail, and he never caused any trouble at home."[30]

Charles E. Lively couldn't avoid a prison sentence for shooting his son, but neither could his family's appeals do anything to allow Gordon to dodge a prison sentence for shooting his father. In addition, it was difficult for Gordon to make the case that the attack on his father was anything other than premeditated, particularly since he repeatedly threatened to get even with the man after he was shot, vows of violence which were quoted in the newspapers. Despite the best efforts of his mother and siblings, Gordon was sentenced to serve eighteen months in Moundsville. He was paroled on December 1, 1939. Three months after his release, Gordon Lively was once again arrested, this time in Ohio, when he and an associate held-up an Akron taxi driver at gunpoint and stole his taxi.[31] When the police arrested them, following a chase and abandonment of the car, the two young men were in possession of a loaded .38 revolver, counterfeit coins, and Gordon's prison release papers.[32] The bogus money in their possession led to the pair being turned over to the FBI.

As far as Lively's relationship with his other children, all was not well between several of them. In his letter to William C. Blizzard, Lively's son, Charles Albert, criticized his late father for leaving their family behind in Matewan, saying "he did not bother to go back," when the former detective gave surprise testimony for the prosecution in Sid Hatfield's murder trial in Williamson and ultimately revealed his secret life.[33] From the document, it also becomes obvious that Charles Albert doubted his father's account of the courthouse slaying, when he said, "Several times I would butter my father up how brave he must

30. *Beckley Raleigh Register*, Beckley, West Virginia, November 9, 1938.
31. *Beckley Raleigh Register*, Beckley, West Virginia, March 11, 1940.
32. *Mansfield News Journal*, Mansfield, Ohio, March 11, 1940.
33. Blizzard, "When Miners March," A letter from Charles A. Lively to William C. Blizzard.

have been. He would throw out that chest and brag that they drew first." Perhaps most telling of all is his closing of the letter, when he made reference to William C. Blizzard's father, Bill Blizzard, who led the Redneck Army. Charles Albert wrote these words: "I know your father was on the right side, as it helped to defeat Industrial Feudalism in this country."[34]

Apparently, those recent acts of domestic violence in 1937 and 1938, all involving her husband, were the last straw in the often-turbulent relationship between Charles and Icie Lively. Divorces between husbands and wives were rare in those times; therefore, it is not surprising that neither of them chose to dissolve their marriage through the courts. Charles E. Lively and Icie were separated from that time forward, only briefly reuniting in the same house mere months before both of their deaths. It is not firmly established whether their later reunion was one of love or simply of convenience.

Charles E. Lively apparently recovered at least a partial use of his arm, because he was recorded to be working as a mine boss in 1940 and later employed by a coal company in Ashland, West Virginia, in 1942. Strangely enough, Charles E. Lively was finally reaping the bitter harvest of the cloak-and-dagger existence he enjoyed over those many years. The former detective, who often chose to live his life isolated and alone, then found himself alone and isolated. Not only did Lively lose his job with Baldwin-Felts; he was faced with the loss of his wife and family. There is no way of knowing if Lively ever truly felt any remorse over the alienation of his family's affection. It is known, however, that nearly everything that Lively ever did value was gone. William G. Baldwin and Thomas L. Felts were dead, passing away in 1936 and 1937, respectively. Perhaps his closest friend in this life, Albert Felts, was shot down in Matewan in 1920. His associates in the courthouse shooting, Hughey Lucas, Bill Salter, and Buster Pence, were all dead by 1932, two of them dying from gunshots to the head, much the same as they administered to Ed Chambers. In short, nothing was left for Lively in West Virginia. After nearly a half-century upon this earth, a man who often chose to live many of those fifty years alone, by then, apparently, had nobody with whom he might share the remainder of his life. But one thing that was undeniably certain in the life of Charles E. Lively was the fact that, in matters regarding the former undercover operative, there were always more secrets yet to be revealed.

---

34. Ibid.

CERTIFICATE OF MARRIAGE
COMMONWEALTH OF VIRGINIA

CITY OR COUNTY OF ___Wise___

FULL NAME OF GROOM ___Charles Livley___   CLERK'S NO. ___237___

PRESENT NAME OF BRIDE ___Ollie Mae Hale___

	GROOM					BRIDE		
AGE	RACE	SINGLE, WIDOWED, OR DIVORCED	NO. TIMES PREV. MARRIED	AGE	RACE	SINGLE, WIDOWED, OR DIVORCED	NO. TIMES PREV. MARRIED
52	W	Div	1	32	W	S	

OCCUPATION ___Mine Boss___   MAIDEN NAME
___Vinton Ill___

BIRTHPLACE ___Russell,___   BIRTHPLACE ___Castlewood, Va___

FATHER'S FULL NAME ___Joe Livley___   FATHER'S FULL NAME ___Buck Hale___

MOTHER'S MAIDEN NAME ___Ameretta Parsons___   MOTHER'S MAIDEN NAME ___Sarah Bradley___

RESIDENCE P.O. ADDRESS (IF IN CITY ST. AND NO.) ___St Paul, Va___   RESIDENCE P.O. ADDRESS (IF IN CITY ST. AND NO.) ___St Paul, Va___

Date of Proposed Marriage ___June 21, 1940___   Place of Proposed Marriage ___Wise, Va___

Given under my hand this ___ day of ___ 19___

CERTIFICATE OF TIME AND PLACE OF MARRIAGE

I, ___ of the ___ Church, or religious order of that name, do certify that on the ___ day of ___ 19___ at ___ Virginia, under authority of this license, I joined together in the Holy State of Matrimony the persons named and described therein. I qualified and gave bond according to law authorizing me to celebrate the rites of marriage in the county (or city) of ___ Commonwealth of Virginia.

Given under my hand this ___ day of ___ 19___

Address of celebrant ___

Lively's illegal marriage certificate to Ollie Mae Hale in 1940, while he was still married to Icie Bell Lively. Please pay special attention to the line indicating Lively's place of birth.

(Courtesy of Jim Miracle)

V.S. Form 50
2-59—15M

STATE FILE NO.

ABSTRACT OF DIVORCE DECREE
COMMONWEALTH OF VIRGINIA
DEPARTMENT OF HEALTH—BUREAU OF VITAL STATISTICS   ___5262___

Place (city or county) ___Roanoke, Va.___   Date of decree ___9-19-61___

Plaintiff ___Charlie Everett Lively___   Age ___73___   Color ___White___

Residence ___2554 Center Av, N.W, Roanoke, Va___   Birthplace ___Vinton, Va.___

Occupation* ___Not Given___   Industry or business ___xx___

Defendant ___Ollie Mae Hale Lively___   Age ___53___   Color ___White___

Residence ___109 Elm Ave, SW, Roanoke, Va.___   Birthplace ___Castlewood, Va.___

Occupation* ___Housewife___   Industry or business ___xx___

Date of marriage ___June 21, 1940___   Place ___Wise, Virginia___

Duration of marriage ___21yrs.2mo.28days___ Number of minor children affected ___None___

Cause of divorce ___parties lived separate and apart for more than 3 years___   Husband ☒ Yes ☐   Yes ☐

Divorce granted to: Wife ☐   Was case contested: No ☒   Alimony granted: No ☒

Kind of divorce ___Absolute___   Signature ___Walker R. Carter___

Date of separation ___September 1955___   Clerk of ___Hustings Court___

Send only Bed and Bd.-Absolute-Annulment
* If wife has no gainful occupation say housewife

All above information as at time of decree

Lively's divorce decree from Ollie Mae Hale.

(Courtesy of Jim Miracle)

Chapter 13

Final Days

As the United States was just emerging from the depths of the Great Depression and Adolf Hitler was waging war on Britain and much of Europe, the coalfields of southern West Virginia were finally and successfully unionized. Charles E. Lively lived long enough to see it. Baldwin-Felts was just a bad memory for coal miners in the state, Don Chafin was no longer sheriff of Logan County, and Lively's anti-union efforts for the Agency had all come to naught. The twilight years of the former, undercover operative's life weren't as turbulent as those of his past, but still, Lively's latter years were also not without their secrets.

After the breakdown of his marriage to Icie Bell Goff, whom he married in 1911, Charles E. Lively was not contented to live his life alone. He also had no apparent interest in terminating his long-standing marriage to the mother of his ten children. There is, however, most certainly a good reason to believe Lively was a womanizer. Perhaps Lively was only guilty of straying outside his marriage one time, but his marital infidelity was clearly not limited to a single instance or merely a brief affair. In fact, it can also be conclusively stated that Lively was a bigamist. The record indicates that Lively met and married a woman twenty years his junior, on June 21, 1940, in Wise, Virginia.[1]

In studying the record of Charles E. Lively, the mysteries and questions concerning the veracities of his life are never ending. According to the Federal Census, taken on April 2, 1940. Lively was a married man, living alone, the resident of a boarding house in McDowell County, West Virginia, and was 48-years-old at his last birthday. On his marriage license, issued nearly two months later, Lively correctly identified himself as 53 years-old. He also stated he was employed as a mine boss and residing in St. Paul, Virginia. Lively married Ollie Mae Hale, without obtaining any divorce decree from his wife, Icie.[2]

---

1. Commonwealth of Virginia, Public Records.
2. Certificate of Marriage, Commonwealth of Virginia, Ancestry. www.ancestry.com.

His new bride, Ollie Mae, was born in Castlewood, Virginia, around 1908. She was the daughter of Buck Hale and Sarah Bradley. Despite being thirty-two years of age, her union with Lively was Ollie Mae's first marriage.

With Lively, his duplicitous nature was never confined to just his detective work; this characteristic obviously permeated every facet of his being. On his second marriage application, Lively falsely listed himself as married one time, but currently divorced. In addition, Lively also exhibited a rare moment of honesty, when he stated that he was born in West Virginia, an inconvenient truth Lively quickly retracted by altering the place of his birth. Lying to the Virginia clerk of courts, Lively, on second thought, brazenly declared he was born in somewhere other than West Virginia. In fact, as one looks at the document, it is plain to see where the clerk originally typed "West Va." as his birthplace and then used the typewriter to cover that information over with repeated key strikes to remove the previous entry. Right above that portion of the altered document, one can see where Lively, born and raised in West Virginia, falsely listed his birthplace as, "Vinton, Illinois."[3]

With these two instances of presenting false information, such as giving a fraudulent birthplace and lying about his marital status, it is clear that Lively knew he was deliberately committing a criminal act. Although the chances of the authorities discovering his concurrent marriages, and punishing him for them, were unlikely for the period, perhaps Lively momentarily reverted back to his former days as an undercover operative, when concealing the truth was essential to his continued survival. It could also be speculated that Lively's dissemblance had just gotten to be a habit with the former detective and he liked it. Ollie Mae is also listed as Lively's contact person, the one "Who Will Always Know Your Address," on his World War II draft registration, which he signed on April 27, 1942, while he was employed by Ashland Coal & Coke Co., and residing at Ashland, West Virginia.[4]

It is not conclusively known whether Charles' wife, Icie, and Ollie Mae knew they each shared the same husband. There are persistent rumors that Charles returned to his home state and occasionally introduced Ollie Mae to people he knew and some family members as "his wife." It has also been said that Icie eventually learned about Ollie Mae's existence. If those rumors

3. Ibid.
4. World War II Draft Registration, Ancestry, www.ancestry.com.

are indeed correct, it cannot be determined whether Ollie Mae also knew the truth about the marital status of Charles and Icie. If Charles E. Lively introduced his newest wife to anyone in the family, however; it is quite likely Icie learned of it also, since gossip often traveled fast in those small West Virginia communities.

In the midst of the 1940s, America had fully entered the war and Charles E. Lively was living in a different state. Charles and Ollie Mae were running the Forde Hotel, in Roanoke, Virginia. "The building, formerly located at 12½ S. Jefferson Street was built in 1883. It was originally known as the Wright Building and housed several different businesses, including retail shops and a printing company. It became the Cox hotel in 1915, the Jefferson Hotel in 1922, and the Forde Hotel in 1940. The building does not appear to have ever been solely a hotel, because other businesses are listed at the same address. It is likely that the second floor comprised the hotel with retail on the street level."[5] It is not known how Lively obtained this hotel position, but it seems that he was always a resourceful man; therefore, it can be speculated that the former detective for Baldwin-Felts, which was also based in Roanoke, took advantage of those long-time agency connections to set himself up as a hotel manager. Perhaps his experiences running a restaurant also served him well in gaining this position.

In 1952, another one of Lively's acquaintances, his boyhood friend, Fred Mooney, died under strange and disturbing circumstances. The former secretary-treasurer of UMWA's District 17 attempted to kill his wife and his children, by placing dynamite under the springs of his wife's cot. After Mooney left home for his job at the Rochester & Pittsburgh Coal Company in Fairmont, West Virginia, an explosion occurred at his residence.

The newspaper reported: "Mrs. Mooney was not seriously injured and the seven children sleeping in the house were unharmed."[6] When Mooney was told about the explosion, "a short time later shot himself with a .38 caliber pistol." The coroner ruled the explosion as an "attempted murder and suicide."[7] It was one more tragic incident where one of the major

---

5. Information supplied to the author by an employee of the Roanoke Public Library, Roanoke, Virginia.
6. *Charleston Daily Mail*, Charleston, West Virginia, February 25, 1952.
7. Ibid.

players in those early twentieth century coal mine wars died from bizarre and bloody circumstances.

On March 21, 1955, Lively applied for Social Security, the brainchild of President Franklin Delano Roosevelt's administration, numbers which made it nearly impossible for an individual to successfully pull off the life of deception that the former detective formerly led. Later that same year, on September 1, Charles E. Lively and Ollie Mae purchased the Bon Vue apartments in Roanoke, at 201 Elm Ave. S.W., a building which still exists. The couple resided there and managed those apartments, selling half of them to a partner on May 17, 1957.[8] There is nothing to suggest that most of those years were not happy ones for the couple. But perhaps lasting happiness and marital bliss were not something in the cards for someone who followed the dark and violent path that Lively walked.

At some point during their marriage, Ollie Mae grew weary of their relationship and decided it was time to leave her husband. The cause of her departure is not clear, but Ollie Mae apparently left their residence somewhere around the beginning of summer in 1958 and never returned.[9] It can be speculated that perhaps her absence occurred when she finally learned of Lively's other wife, and became angry with the former detective for concealing that information. Ollie Mae had no way of knowing, however, that the keeping of secrets had always been Lively's stock-in-trade.

Perhaps Ollie Mae simply met and fell in love with someone else, speculation with some basis in fact because she once again returned to the marriage altar only three short months after their divorce. In addition, it is known that Lively was going blind and perhaps Ollie Mae balked at the possibility of being his caretaker.[10] Whatever might have been Ollie Mae's reason for leaving, her three-year absence caused Charles to file for divorce in September 1961, for which he cited the following cause: "Parties lived separate and apart for more than 3 years."[11] Apparently, in the mind of the former detective, extended absences from the home were only acceptable for the husband. Their Virginia divorce decree marked the conclusion to a twenty-

---

8. Information supplied to the author by an employee of the Roanoke Public Library, Roanoke, Virginia.
9. Abstract of Divorce Decree, Commonwealth of Virginia, Department of Health, Bureau of Vital Statistics.
10. *Raleigh Register*, Beckley, West Virginia, May 31, 1962.
11. Divorce Decree, Commonwealth of Virginia, Bureau of Vital Statistics, Ancestry, www.ancestry.com.

one-year period in the former detective's life when Charles E. Lively was illegally married to two women at the same time.

Following his divorce from Ollie Mae, Lively once again returned to the state of West Virginia in September 1961. It is not known why his wife, Icie, consented to take him back and allowed Lively to move into the house with her. Their initial parting was certainly less than amicable. Perhaps his wife's decision was only based on pity for the former detective, since it is documented that Charles had gone blind. Whatever the reason, Lively successfully engineered some kind of reunification with his wife and moved into her modest home at 1917 McVeigh Avenue, Huntington, West Virginia.

All his life, Lively had been a fiercely proud individual, doing what he chose, showing no fear in regards to the consequences of his actions. But proud men are often not good medical patients; they also impulsively spurn the idea of subjecting themselves to the mercy of others. No longer was Lively a Baldwin-Felts agent, nor the dangerous man he once had been. Charles E. Lively was blind and in need of a caretaker. In addition, Icie was also suffering from several serious health issues of her own. The record indicates that Icie was confined to a hospital in late May, perhaps leaving the former detective to care for his needs himself. It is not at all surprising that a man who lived the life that Lively experienced would not choose to leave this world in a conventional manner.

In fact, his fate was strikingly similar to that of his boyhood friend, Fred Mooney, ten years earlier. Lively elected to end his life in much the same way he lived, with a gun in his hand. On May 28, 1962, Charles E. Lively took his revolver, held it to his skull, and squeezed the trigger. The former Baldwin-Felts agent drew his final breath right there on the floor of their meager Huntington home. Charles E. Lively died alone.

Having shot his son, Gordon previously, this was not the first time that Lively had stained the floors of Icie's residence with the blood of a family member. It was, however; the final time Lively left others to clean up the mess he often left behind. A portion of his obituary read: "Lively died Monday afternoon at his home of a self-inflicted wound to his head. Cabell County Coroner Robert S. Barrett termed the death suicide, after investigating officers found a .38 caliber pistol in the victim's hand. Huntington Police Sgt. Ted Barr said powder burns found on one hand indicated the pistol was gripped tightly as it was fired. A daughter, Mrs. Gladys Jenkins, MacArthur [West

Virginia], said the weapon was apparently the pistol her father used when he was a well-known detective in various parts of the United States. She noted he had been blind for over a year."[12]

There is every reason to believe that Lively's suicide was not an impulsive and thoughtless act. Moreover, it is very probable that his death may have been carefully planned by the detective some months earlier. On January 12, 1962, Lively went to a lawyer to draw up his will, which revealed a couple of things about this complex and deeply troubled man.

The detective's hand writing, when he signed his signature to the document, was obviously that of man who was suffering from a loss of eyesight. Despite the rancor he had with much of his family, he apparently had no less than a cordial relationship with his youngest son, Paul, who Lively listed as "my beloved son." Lively also selected Paul as the executor of his estate. When Lively died, he owned fifty-one shares of Appalachian Power Company stock and his estate received the payment from his partners in Roanoke, on the Bon Vue Apartments.[13]

Perhaps, at the end, revealing that his heart wasn't totally made out of stone, Charles E. Lively closed his last will and testament with this third point: "All the rest and residue of my estate, both real and personal, of whatever and whenever situate, which I now own or may hereafter acquire and belonging to me at the time of my death, I do hereby give, bequeath, and devise unto my beloved wife, Icie B. Lively."[14]

The former Baldwin-Felts detective, after his debts were paid, left behind the sum of $17,487.88 to his wife. Icie Lively, who was already in bad health, however, would not greatly improve her station in life from her husband's estate. Icie only outlived her late husband by a few months, passing away on November 25, 1962, from a heart attack. Unlike her husband's obituary, which mentioned only a wife and pair of daughters as his survivors when he committed suicide, Icie B. Lively's obituary listed her survivors as six sons and three daughters. Perhaps in one final act of casual disregard for the unorthodox life of their troubled and often absent father, the obituary listed Charles E. Lively's passing on the wrong date.

---

12. *Raleigh Register*, Beckley, West Virginia, May 31, 1962.
13. Last Will and Testament for Charlie E. Lively, Clerk of Courts, Cabell County, West Virginia.
14. Ibid.

The house in Huntington, West Virginia, where Lively committed suicide.

(Author's collection)

Epilogue

Although it's been almost one hundred years since the bloodshed in La Veta, Ludlow, Matewan, and Welch, the names of William G. Baldwin, Thomas L Felts, and, yes, Charles E. Lively can still stir an extraordinary level of hatred among those same coal mining communities. From the record, it's clear that Lively murdered no fewer than three, unarmed men in his lifetime, one in Colorado and two in West Virginia. It also appears that killing was something that came easy for him. Taking into account Lively's missing and undocumented years in Oklahoma, Missouri, Kansas, and Illinois, while working for Baldwin-Felts, it's quite likely his personal death toll may have been much higher. Moreover, Lively's legendary scrapbook cannot be counted upon to shed any light on these years, either.

William G. Baldwin's great grandson, James Baldwin has stated that the scrapbook Lively kept of his exploits is no longer fully intact. It is rumored that, in a fit of anger from learning about her husband's other wife, Icie began ripping pages from the book and tossing them into a fire, until a family member came along and stopped her. Baldwin further claims that there is nothing left of Lively's scrapbook before the year 1922, which precludes learning any more about Lively's mysterious years in the West.

All of those individuals who Lively is known to have killed, were shot down at the request, or with the implicit knowledge, of his superiors at Baldwin-Felts. For one of those murders, Lively spent approximately sixteen months behind bars, after pleading guilty to involuntary manslaughter. Yet, despite this knowledge, Baldwin-Felts still chose to keep this man in their employ. That action smacks of complicity. Perhaps it was intended to be a lesson to all those who dared to cross the agency in the future.

There can be no question that Charles E. Lively lied while taking his oath to the UMWA and also to the Western Federation of Miners, and often perjured himself in his instances of court testimony. The detective pistol-whipped at least one individual in a fit of anger. He was accused and later acquitted of raping a young girl. Lively beat his wife and children with a phone cord and even locked one of them in the cellar. He once ordered the company store to give his wife and children no food or provisions. If that wasn't enough, Charles E. Lively shot, either by accident or with clear intent, his own son, Gordon. Lively was a harsh and violent man, an individual of sudden and extreme urges. In addition, for twenty-one years, Lively was even married to two women at the same time.

Perhaps the best thing that can be said about Charles. E. Lively is there can be no question that he was extremely dedicated and fiercely loyal to the men who employed him and to the work which he did for Baldwin-Felts. Moreover, even long after his services to the Agency were terminated, Lively still prominently displayed pictures of Baldwin and Felts on his mantel, an almost sacred place in most homes, normally reserved for friends, loved ones, and those with the closest relationships to the homeowner. However, that should also explain the value Lively placed upon those men in his own life.

Even a century after the killings in Matewan, the questions still remain. Was Charles E. Lively merely a mercenary, influenced only by his desire for money and little else? Or was Lively also a loyal soldier in the anti-union forces? It is quite likely, however, that he was indeed both. There can be no question of his loyalty and dedication to the job. He had already spent sixteen months in a Colorado jail cell, because Baldwin-Felts required it. In order to please the agency, Lively was willing to kill two, unarmed men in broad daylight, in front of a host of witnesses. Although it is certain that he may have believed the wealth of the coal companies and the prominence of Thomas Felts made it likely the jury would ultimately be stacked in his favor, Lively still had no guarantees he wouldn't be found guilty, face many more months in jail, or worse still, swing from a hangman's rope. At the same time, Lively also believed his actions were fully justified. His late son, Paul Lively once said in an interview, "He thought he was doing his bit to keep Communism out of this country."[1]

Putting Lively under a microscope is indeed a complicated task. To do so, it became necessary to consult with mental health authorities, who studied his words and habits, the actions he took, and what those most closely associated with Lively had to say about him:

---

1. Topper Sherwood, "The Killings Continue," "Wild, Wonderful West Virginia," February 1991, pp. 26-31.

"While reviewing the information that I was given concerning Mr. Lively, and after examination of this information, I have come to the conclusion that Mr. Charles Lively exhibited Sociopathic traits. Lively often presented as overly calm in scary and uncertain situations, had very few friends and no close loving relationships, even though he was married and had children and presented as a loyal, loving relationship at times. He was often found to be deceitful, arrogant, hostile, aggressive, and impulsive. He is described as narcissistic with a strong lack of empathy, "cold hearted", manipulative, but could be very charming. Mr. Lively was clearly, in my professional opinion, a Sociopath."

Evaluated by: Therese Bombardiere, BS Psychology AS Criminal Justice. AS Nursing. Ms. Bombardiere has over 17 years' experience in the field of Psychology and previously employed as a Registered Nurse for nearly 20 years.

Perhaps Lively was the victim of a bad home life. Maybe he was little more than a product of extreme poverty and difficult working conditions. It is, however, patently unfair to measure Charles E. Lively by anything other than the yardstick of his own times. But how does one explain the bizarre deaths of both Lively and his boyhood friend, Fred Mooney, raised in the same community? What is it about such men that explains their actions and, ultimately, their ends?

Lively shot and perhaps intended to kill his own son; Mooney plotted to kill both his own wife and children. Both of these boyhood friends, who grew to be adult adversaries, took their own lives with a gun. Those incidents leave some to wonder if the environment in which Lively and Mooney were raised was destined to become an incubator for violence and bloodshed. Perhaps the abject poverty and wanton violence visited upon striking miners by the powerful coal companies of that day also served to somehow devalue human life in the hearts and minds of these men, rising to the point where they no longer cared or placed any value whatsoever on their own lives or upon those of their fellow men? Those questions may never be answered.

From the nature of his work, and the zeal by which he approached it, it is evident that Charles E. Lively was a man unhindered by the normal inhibitions of human conscience. There is nothing in the sociopathic behavior of Charles E. Lively that would give any indication that the former detective ever displayed any sense of remorse, or was suddenly overtaken by guilt, qualities which might have caused him to regret his actions enough to take his own life at seventy-five years of age. As a result of a Freedom of Information request, it is known that the police department in Huntington, West Virginia, no longer has any records involving their investigation of Lively's suicide. Therefore, nothing more can be gleaned from Lively's final act in this life.

His was certainly a remarkable life, one deserving to be chronicled, and much too extraordinary to be fictionalized. Despite his activities and misdeeds, despite the danger he faced, despite the number of enemies Lively earned, the deadliest man in the West Virginia-Colorado coal mine wars outlived nearly all of his contemporaries, friends and foes alike. Only Frank Keeney, the former USW District 17 president who died peaceably in 1970, eclipsed Lively.

From the record, it becomes clear that Charles E. Lively was not a good man, but his life was most certainly an intriguing one. "Neither the union nor the coal operators were lily white back then," the late Paul Lively once told an interviewer.[2] He was certainly correct. Paul's father was a major player in a deadly and extended drama which had very few heroes, and no white hats. There is no doubt that there is still much about Lively which the world may never know. After living so many of his years in the shadows, and with much of his life and career forever shrouded in mystery, one has to believe this is the way that Charles E. Lively would have wanted it.

---

2. Ibid.

Appendix A

Author's commentary on Matewan Shootout

In no less than two of the most prominent books regarding the Matewan Massacre, the authors went to great pains to emphatically state that only three or four of the detectives were licensed and carrying pistols when the violence occurred in Matewan, West Virginia, on May 19, 1920. Those individuals were Albert Felts, Lee Felts, C.B. Cunningham, and Bill Salter. According to Velke and Lee, the other nine detectives were essentially unarmed, only carrying their rifles and pistols in cases. This, however, cannot in any way be an accurate recounting of the facts. Not only did the Felts brothers, Cunningham, and Salter have pistols, there is also sworn testimony that A.J. Boorher did some shooting as well. Also, how was Detective Boorher shooting a cased weapon? In addition, John McDowell also testified in the Williamson, West Virginia, trial that he fired two or three shots himself, making it unlikely that he was not illegally carrying a pistol as well. With those facts in mind, it is certainly not unreasonable to conclude that some of the other detectives may have also been carrying concealed weapons while waiting for the train that rainy afternoon. It is known that some of them were wearing rain coats, which may have masked the pistol bulges under their coats. Although the detectives were decidedly outnumbered and outgunned on the streets that fateful day, it is pure fiction to suggest that those thirteen Baldwin-Felts Detectives were simply a bunch of helpless and innocent victims, honorable men who were preyed upon while doing their best to zealously uphold the law. The facts clearly show otherwise. As to the matter of whether the thirteen agents were deliberately ambushed by Sid Hatfield and the other armed townspeople, the record clearly shows that they were.

Appendix B

Author's Commentary on McDowell Court House Shootout

If these Baldwin-Felts agents were not there at the courthouse to kill Hatfield and Chambers, then why were they there? Since Lively was the source of the indictment, then he may have had a good reason to be at the courthouse, had there been a trial. But what of Pence, Salter, and Lucas? These three agents had no legitimate reason to be at the courthouse in Welch on that day. Moreover, they also could provide no testimony regarding the incident at Mohawk. Pence claimed that he didn't even know Lively at the time of the shooting. So, why did he choose that one particular day, in that one particular place, to be in that spot to clean his nails? If Pence had nothing to offer in regards to this case, why did he assume that Hatfield and Chambers were allegedly shooting at him? Salter claimed that he was inside the courthouse and fired no shots, but it is known Salter spoke to Sallie Chambers on the courthouse steps immediately upon the slaying of her husband. One also has to wonder to what purpose Hughey Lucas was there. The record leaves us to presume Lucas' role was to provide the throwaway weapon with the six spent cartridges, which was placed in or near the hands of Hatfield and Chambers. These Baldwin-Felts agents, acting under their status as McDowell County deputy sheriffs gave them a cover story and the ultimate authority to be at the courthouse, fully armed. That information also destroys the credibility of Buster Pence's testimony, making it unlikely that Pence wouldn't know Charles E, Lively, his fellow deputy sheriff, or the identities of the others agents/deputies involved in the shooting.

BIBLIOGRAPHY

Primary Sources:

Blizzard, William C. and Bill. "When Miners March" Coal and Labor Collection, Appalachian Collection, McConnell Library, Radford University, Radford, VA.

Blizzard, William C., and Wess Harris. *When Miners March*. Oakland, CA: PM Press, 2010.

Corbin, David A., editor. *Gun Thugs, Rednecks, and Radicals: A Documentary History of the West Virginia Mine Wars*. Oakland, CA: PM Press, 2011.

Eastern Regional Coal Archives, Craft Memorial Library, Bluefield, West Virginia: Thomas L. Felts Papers.

Matewan, People Of. *Better World: Testimony To Congress on the Matewan Massacre: 1920/1921*. Edited by Ryan K. Hardesty. Privately Published, 2018.

Mooney, Fred. *Struggle in the Coal Fields, The Autobiography of Fred Mooney*. Morgantown, WV: West Virginia University Library, 1967.

United States Commission on Industrial Relations. *Industrial Relations: Final Report and Testimony, Volume 7*. Washington: D.C. Government Printing Office, 1916.

Newspapers

Athens Messenger, Athens, Ohio
Beckley Post Herald, Beckley, West Virginia
Beckley Raleigh Register, Beckley, West Virginia
Beckley Sunday Register, Beckley, West Virginia
Bluefield Daily Telegraph, Bluefield, West Virginia
Bradford Era, Bradford, Pennsylvania
Burlington Daily Hawk Eye Gazette, Burlington, Iowa
Charleston Gazette-Mail, Charleston, West Virginia
Colorado Springs Gazette, Colorado Springs, Colorado
The Cedar Rapids Evening Gazette, Cedar Rapids, Iowa
Del Norte San Juan Prospector, Del Norte, Colorado
Eagle Valley Enterprise, Eagle, Colorado
East Liverpool Evening Review, East Liverpool, Ohio
Fort Wayne Journal Gazette, Fort Wayne, Indiana
Galveston Tribune, Galveston, Texas
Gettysburg Times, Gettysburg, Pennsylvania
Hattiesburg American, Hattiesburg, Mississippi
Helena Weekly Independent, Helena, Montana
Jacksonville Daily Illinois Courier, Jacksonville, Illinois
Joplin Globe, Joplin, Missouri
The Kingsport Times, Kingsport, Tennessee
Leadville Herald Democrat, Leadville, Colorado
Logansport Pharos Tribune, Logansport, Indiana
Montrose Daily Press, Montrose, Colorado
Muskogee Times Democrat, Muskogee, Oklahoma
Nevada State Journal, Reno, Nevada
The New York Times
Ogden Standard-Examiner, Ogden, Utah
Phoenix Arizona Republican, Phoenix, Arizona
Roanoke World News, Roanoke, Virginia
Walsenburg World, Walsenburg, Colorado
Washington C.H. Daily Record, Washington Court House, Ohio
Welch Daily News, Welch, West Virginia
Xenia Evening Gazette, Xenia, Ohio

Secondary Books:

Bailey, Rebecca J. *Matewan Before the Massacre: Politics, Coal, and the Roots of Conflict in a West Virginia Mining Community*. Morgantown: West Virginia University Press, 2008.

Corbin, David. *Life, Work, and Rebellion in the Coal Fields: The Southern West Virginia Miners, 1880-1922*. Champaign: University of Illinois Press, 1981.

Green, James. *The Devil Is Here in These Hills: West Virginia's Coal Miners and Their Battle for Freedom*. New York: Atlantic Monthly Press, 2015.

Hall, Ronald W. *The Carroll County Courthouse Tragedy*. Hillsville, VA: The Carroll County Historical Society, 2018.

Kline, Michael, with Wess Harris, editor. *Written in Blood: Courage and Corruption in the Appalachian War of Extraction*. Oakland, CA: PM Press, 2017.

Lee, Howard B. *Bloodletting in Appalachia: the story of West Virginia's four major mine wars and other thrilling incidents of its coal fields*. Parsons, WV: McClain Printing Company, 1969.

Martelle, Scott. *Blood Passion: The Ludlow Massacre and Class War in the American West*. Chicago: Rutgers University Press, 2008.

McGovern, George S., and Leonard F. Guttridge. *The Great Coalfield War*. New York: Houghton Mifflin, 1972.

Ree, Dorothy. *Walsenburg - Crossroads Town*. Morrisville: Lulu.com, 2006.

Savage, Lon. *Thunder In the Mountains: The West Virginia Mine War, 1920–21*. University of Pittsburgh: University of Pittsburgh Press, 1990.

Shogan, Robert. *The Battle of Blair Mountain: The Story of America's Largest Labor Uprising*. New York: Basic Books, 2006.

Sullivan, Ken. *The Goldenseal book of the West Virginia mine wars: articles reprinted from Goldenseal magazine, 1977-1991*. Missoula, MT: Pictorial Histories Publishing Company, 1991.

Velke, John A. *The True Story of the Baldwin-Felts Detective Agency*. Privately published, 2004.

Secondary Articles:

Fort Wayne Journal-Gazette. "Hired Deputies Without Regard To Qualification." December 10, 1914, 1,13.

"Hellraisers Journal: They Call It the Kingdom of Farr, Through the Influence of the CF&I Company." *Daily Kos.* Last modified December 11, 2014. https://www.dailykos.com/stories/2014/12/11/1350811/-Hellraisers-Journal-They-call-it-the-Kingdom-of-Farr-through-the-influence-of-the-CF-I-Company.

Lively, Gerald. "Exploitation, Duplicity, Corrpution, and Domestic Warfare - the West Virginia Coal Industry." *Daily Kos.* Last modified January 18, 2014. https://www.dailykos.com/stories/2014/1/18/1270728/-Exploitation-duplicity-corrpution-and-domestic-warfare-the-West-Virginia-coal-industry.

Websites and Databases

"A People's History of the Spanish Peaks." *Spanish Peaks County - Explore Southern Colorado's Rich History, Natural Wonders, and Artistic Inspiration,* 17 Apr. 2019, spanishpeakscountry.com/a-peoples-history-of-the-spanish-peaks/.

Colorado Digitization Program. "Colorado Coal Field War Project." University of Denver, Colorado Digitization Program, www.du.edu/ludlow/cfhist.html.

"Steeped in History." "City of Walsenburg—A Great Place to Be." https://www.colorado.gov/walsenburg. November 11, 2019.

Index

About the Author

R.G. Yoho is a West Virginia native with a passion for history and tales of the American West. A proud member of the Western Writers of America, he's the author of seven Westerns and several nonfiction works. Yoho is also the current President of the West Virginia Writers, Inc. For more about the author, visit his website: www.RGYoho.com.